# checklists for entrepreneurs

## Your shortcut to success

Robert Ashton

**Prentice Hall**
is an imprint of

Harlow, England • London • New York • Boston • San Francisco • Toronto
Sydney • Tokyo • Singapore • Hong Kong • Seoul • Taipei • New Delhi
Cape Town • Madrid • Mexico City • Amsterdam • Munich • Paris • Milan

PEARSON EDUCATION LIMITED
Edinburgh Gate
Harlow CM20 2JE
Tel: +44 (0)1279 623623
Fax: +44 (0)1279 431059
Website: www.pearsoned.co.uk

First published 2004 (published as *The Entrepreneur's Book of Checklists*)
Second edition 2007 (published as *The Entrepreneur's Book of Checklists*)
**Third edition 2010 (published as *Brilliant Checklists for Entrepreneurs*)**

© Pearson Education Limited 2004, 2007, 2010

The right of Robert Ashton to be identified as author of this work has been
asserted by him in accordance with the Copyright, Designs and Patents Act 1988.

Pearson Education is not responsible for the content of third party internet sites.

ISBN 978-0-273-74080-3

*British Library Cataloguing in Publication Data*
A CIP catalogue record for this book can be obtained from the British Library.

*Library of Congress Cataloging-in-Publication Data*
Ashton, Robert, 1955-
   Brilliant checklists for entrepreneurs : your shortcut to success /
Robert Ashton. -- 3rd ed.
      p. cm.
   ISBN 978-0-273-74080-3 (pbk.)
 1. New business enterprises. 2. Entrepreneurship. 3. Success in
business. I. Title.
   HD62.5.A815 2010
   658.4'09--dc22

                                                              2010029062

ARP Impression 98

Typeset in 10.5pt/11.5pt Plantin by 30
Printed in Great Britain by Clays Ltd, St Ives plc

*This book is dedicated to my wife Belinda, my son Tom and my daughter Ruth. Entrepreneurship is exciting, stimulating and rewarding, but almost impossible without the support of a loving family. However hard you work at starting and growing your enterprise, always make time for your family.*

# About the author

**Robert Ashton** describes himself as 'the barefoot entrepreneur'. He says that's because to succeed today you need to be sensitive to those around you, in touch with reality and to tread gently as you grow your business.

Others describe him as a very human entrepreneur: authentic, genuine, honest and at times quite humble. He's started three companies and helped found a charity. He believes that entrepreneurship is as much an attitude as a skill. As a best-selling author, popular business speaker and often outspoken commentator, he makes entrepreneurship accessible, understandable and, above all, possible for everyone who wants to give it a try. Quite simply he says it like it is: simply, clearly and memorably.

Robert works with entrepreneurs who want to make the world a better place. Providing they are passionate, committed and convinced that what they plan is going to benefit others as well as themselves, he'll help if he can. You can contact Robert via his website **www.robertashton.co.uk** or by email: **robert@robertashton.co.uk**.

# Contents

# Introduction

I t doesn't matter what prompted you to start or grow your business. Neither does it matter if your focus is lifestyle, making a difference, profit alone or even global domination. The challenges you face will be just the same. Under the skin, every organisation needs to be well managed, sustainable and really understand its customers.

This book is not a boring business manual. Instead it is an extensive compendium of proven tips. There's nothing here that's not been tried and found to work. There's little that will prove costly to try and much that will take you past the pitfalls we all encounter.

Some of you will start at the beginning and read the book through to the end. Others will dip in and out as the need arises. All of you will discover things to do, ideas to try and at times stuff that will make you laugh. Business, after all, does have to be fun too!

Here are ten good reasons for reading further.

1  **Ideas** – are you seeking inspiration or are you still searching for your killer business idea? This book shows you how to create and test business ideas.

2  **Risk** – all change involves risk, but the potential rewards are immense. Discover answers to the questions you've not yet thought of asking. Minimise your risk and maximise your return.

3  **Goals** – what do you really want from your business? See how setting lifestyle goals will help you focus your business vision.

4  **Cash** – finding the money is never simple; this book lists places to look that you've probably never thought of. Banks are not your only option!

5   **Customers** – if your business is not growing, it's probably shrinking! Find out how to manage the flow of new customers and keep control of your sales and profits.

6   **Visibility** – the easier you are to find, the more products or services you will sell. Discover how marketing needn't cost much money at all.

7   **Time** – are you running so fast you might trip and fall? Learn how to manage your time and, just as importantly, the time of those around you.

8   **Payment** – do people keep you waiting for money? Cash flow is the life-blood of business growth. This book will give you the confidence and skill to always get paid.

9   **Internet** – it's never been more important to be online with your enterprise. Find out where to spend your time and where to avoid. Succeed online.

10  **Exit** – at some point you'll want to cash in and sell up. This book tells you how.

This book is a practical guide to help you through the many challenges that we all face when we plan, start, grow and sell a business. Each checklist deals with a different topic, listing things to consider and things to try. The book is quick and easy to navigate and completely free from jargon. It's been written for busy people who want a shortcut to inspiration and ideas. It is perfect if you:

- want to start your own business;
- have a business you want to grow;
- are studying enterprise and want a practical book that says it like it really is;
- run a charity or social enterprise and want to become more sustainable;
- advise small business owners and want a handy, no-nonsense guide;
- teach people about enterprise in all its forms;
- find business books hard to read – this book is written to be easy to read;
- live with someone growing a business and want to help;
- sell to small businesses and want to see the world through their eyes;
- want a book that delivers value for money straight away!

Many of the key points in the book are illustrated with case studies. All are the experiences of real people, although some have asked for their names to be changed.

## CHAPTER 1

# Be ambitious

Set your sights at the
right level

# 10 ways to think of your business idea

The most important thing to do is to find time and space to think creatively. You need to create opportunities to take your mind off the day-to-day stuff and contemplate your future. This is just as important whether you're starting a business or planning a change of direction. Here are ten good ways to think about your new idea.

1  **Daydream** – the best ideas always pop up when you're not expecting them. Make time for quiet moments when you can close your eyes and let your mind drift. Let your subconscious mind look for the answers. You'll be surprised at what this can reveal.

2  **Share** – encourage those close to you to think about the opportunities too. Parents, partners, friends and also your children; all have a knack of knowing us better than we think. Let their insight into your strengths guide you through the creative process.

3  **Clear your diary** – you're a busy person. You might need to make sacrifices to free up the time to be creative.

4  **Make lists** – it has to be said that making lists helps. The longer your list of options, the more likely it is to contain some winners. Remember that the ideas you list might not be the right ones themselves, but they may well lead you in the right direction.

5  **Google** – once you've had a good idea, search online for a business already doing it. There's little that's really new and you will get lots of ideas by looking at what others are already doing.

6  **Buy a notebook** – keep it in your pocket, beside the bed and everywhere you go. Ideas can strike at any time. Write them down.

7  **Beware of the hobby habit** – many people feel their hobby holds the key to a successful enterprise. They may be right, but more often they're not. Are there enough people who share your passion with money to spend?

8  **Seasons** – will your idea appeal to your customers all year round? Selling Christmas decorations or hiring out bikes might not keep you afloat on their own. Running two seasonal businesses might.

9  **Check your CV** – some of the most successful people start a business in a marketplace they already know. This shortens the learning curve and usually delivers some easy wins too.

10  **Travel** – you don't need to go far. Visit local trade fairs and see what is promoted there. Pose as a buyer and ask questions. Compare your business vision with what you see and hear. How can you do better?

Every big business was once small. Equally, businesses often change direction completely, in response to changing market demand. Whitbread, for example, was once a major brewer. Now it primarily owns budget hotels and coffee shops. Many would agree that people use coffee shops today as their parents once used pubs. The company has moved with the times, adapting as customer behaviour has evolved.

## brilliant tip

- Try to improve on what's being done already rather than seeking something new.
- Start with a business you know well and look around the fringes for your opportunity.
- Don't just research online; go and talk to people.

## brilliant example

### Mah Hussain-Gambles, Saaf Skincare Products

Disillusioned by the bold claims made by makers of beauty products, Mah decided to create her own range. 'I wanted something I would be happy recommending to my family and friends,' she said. Already a qualified homeopath and pharmacologist, with clinical trials experience, Mah knew how to research and test the products she wanted to formulate and market.

What she created was a range of organic, ethical and effective products that could also be Halal certified. This was a real bonus as many Muslim women are worried about what might be in the skincare products they are using.

The strength of Mah's business idea is that it takes her technical expertise and applies it in a new way. Furthermore, while all women will enjoy using her products, they will appeal especially to Muslim women. Not surprisingly, in 2009, five years after setting up her business, Mah was voted one of Britain's 'Most Enterprising Women' by *Real Business* magazine.

# 10 proven tips on creative thinking

There are countless books on creative thinking. Most promote a particular technique, yet in reality creative thinking is very simple. We find it difficult because we think it's difficult. It is true to say that if you are left handed and therefore right brained, creativity will come to you more naturally. But much more important is a willingness to let go and let your brain run free. Here are ten very simple tips to help you think more creatively.

1   **Close your eyes** – it's harder to see what might be when surrounded by what already exists. Closing your eyes encourages the brain to think more abstractly – to see what might be.

2   **Stretch** – extend your line of thinking beyond the obvious. For example, if it rained all day every day, how would we stay dry? Keep going and you might invent a better umbrella!

3   **The ridiculous** – today's ridiculous is tomorrow's innovation. Twenty years ago, cameras on phones would have been laughed at. Look for parallels in a business sector you know.

4   **Mind maps™** – Tony Buzan has helped countless people become more creative by introducing them to mind mapping. It's a lateral rather than linear way to make notes. Try it.

5   **Context** – you'll often find that what works in one place can be adapted to work elsewhere. Look for your answers in less than obvious places. For example, road workers wear high visibility jackets for safety reasons. Could high visibility clothing become popular in night clubs, where it's dark and difficult to find your friend?

6   **Sleep on it** – it is true that if you ponder on a problem late at night, your subconscious mind will often work out some solutions while you sleep.

7   **Two heads** – creative thinking in a group can sometimes get you answers faster. Use a whiteboard, flipchart or just large sheets of paper to write down what you each think. Other people's ideas will accelerate your own creative thinking.

8   **Return** – don't try to complete the process in one go. Sometimes it's good to put your emerging idea to one side and pick it up again later. You'll see things afresh that way.

9 **Exercise** – do your creative thinking on the move. Even a brisk walk increases your heart rate and the blood flow to your brain. Exercise can fuel creativity.

10 **Chocolate** – we all need the excuse to indulge ourselves so why not make your creative thinking sessions special by allowing yourself some treats?

Creativity is really little more than thinking beyond the obvious or presenting familiar things in new ways. In enterprise, creativity is important because you constantly have new barriers to overcome. Competitors, customers and your own curiosity will prompt you to think creatively about what you do.

## Everything is new when you see it for the first time

We can usually remember vividly our first day at school. It's a big change and, for many, rather frightening. Yet every year children start school for the first time. The teachers have seen it all before, but for their students it's a completely new experience.

When you're thinking creatively, remember that what you offer people doesn't have to be totally new. It only has to be new to them.

 **brilliant** **example**

**Toby Buckle, Hazelbranch Coaching and Training**

Toby runs his own business coaching practice and so helps others with their creativity. However, even the experts sometimes need help to step back and view their enterprise objectively. Taking time off when his daughter was born helped him realise how he'd dropped into the comfort of following what he called his business 'auto-pilot', simply doing what he'd always done. He said it was like driving without satnav, where you had to read road signs and think about where you were going.

Too many of us simply follow the voice on the dashboard and forget to use our instincts and intuition. Make regular time for creative thinking and never simply do what others suggest unless you're really sure.

# 10 things you need to be honest with yourself about

You'll get plenty of advice to help you avoid being fooled by others but little on how to avoid being fooled by yourself. Few business advisers have the courage to challenge your motives or your abilities. Starting a business is not for everyone.

If you have a business already and are looking to grow it, you need to ask yourself why. Just as some people are happier working for others, so many are happy running a small business. Building a business can sound appealing, but it might not actually make you any happier or richer.

Here are ten things to consider before you embark on the next step in your enterprise journey. Be honest with yourself and recognise that we're all different. A business is like a jacket – one size does not fit all.

1　**Life goals** – your enterprise should be the vehicle that can carry you to where you want to go. Work out what you want from your life before doing the same for your business.

2　**Money** – take time to explore and really understand your attitude to money. It's essential to keep house and home together, but once you have enough, more may not make life any better. Only set out to make a million if a million will buy what you really want.

3　**Values** – we are all the product of our parentage and our past. Some people find the very concept of commercial gain abhorrent. Others will gladly exploit others to benefit themselves. Know your values and don't compromise them for your enterprise.

4　**Family** – most entrepreneurs with families find it difficult to balance life and work. In fact most will say that life is work. Make sure you have your family on your side.

5　**Health** – you don't always need good health to succeed in business. However, you do need to choose or develop a business that fits within your physical and mental health limits.

6　**Growth** – it's true to say that you always need to be growing your business, but that's because you'll always be losing customers and will need to replace them. However, don't go for growth for growth's sake, whoever tells you it's a thing you have to do.

7    **Recognition** – we all like to have our successes recognised. Realise, however, that the person you really have to win over is yourself. Many successful businesses have gone bust because the owner became more focused on winning business awards than on the business itself.

8    **Your ceiling** – we all have differing levels of ability. Just as corporate careers peak when you reach the limit of your potential, so too will your own business. Don't try to become someone you're not. Value being who and what you are.

9    **Timescale** – think seriously about your age and how many years you want to do what you're doing or planning now. If you're in a hurry, consider teaming up with someone else or buying into an established enterprise. Each business has an optimum development rate that it's wise not to exceed.

10   **Exit** – finally, remember that for most commercial enterprises the biggest opportunity for wealth creation comes when you sell. Work out what you want to sell your enterprise for and when. Then work towards that goal from day one.

## brilliant tip

**Let your business reflect your values, personality and style**

Society has moved on from the time when business had to be impersonal. Most would now accept that people buy people first and their company second.
Think about how the Virgin group of companies successfully projects Sir Richard Branson's personal values. Ask yourself how you can make your business do the same for you.

## brilliant example

**Samantha McKenna, Voice Brand Design**

Sam had worked for big city-based marketing agencies and had become increasingly disillusioned with the way that conventional agencies operated.

In 2008 she decided to follow her heart and leave the city to create with her partner a specialist agency in rural Leicestershire. They recruited a team who shared their outlook and work with clients to deliver graphic design, print and websites with what she describes as 'impassioned focus'.

It is this emotional dimension that makes a difference. They can now feel they are doing something that really matters and their clients know that they care. Sam has seen her business grow dramatically over the past year. She has proved to herself and others that following your instinct and vision need not hold you back. In Sam's case it has helped her achieve greater success than if she'd remained an employee.

# 10 things to check before chucking in your job

Before you throw away a promising career to start up on your own current business focus, it's good to pause and take an objective look at the job you might be about to leave. Entrepreneurship is not for everyone. Here are some things to consider before jumping ship.

## Five questions to ask yourself about your job

1   Have I explored the option of buying into the company I work for? Perhaps the boss wants to retire and you could buy an increasing share of the business over time.

2   Am I physically and mentally strong enough for the challenge of enterprise? Why not invest in a private medical check-up just to make sure?

3   Do I have a company pension scheme that will pay out significantly less if I leave now? Can I negotiate an early retirement deal and have some pension income while I start my business?

4   I actually like work, so is my life partner pushing me into something I'm not totally sure I want to do? Maybe they should start the business instead.

5   Have I learned all I need to know at work? Perhaps your employer is funding an MBA and it's given you itchy feet! Write your plan by all means but wait until you get the piece of paper before resigning.

## Five questions to help you see your situation objectively

1   Is my boss a control freak who'll never let go? If work is uncomfortable and you think you can do better on your own, it's often worth giving it a go.

2   Is the firm going bust? If it is, you might be able to raise the finance to buy the assets from the receiver and get off to a flying start with the business you already know.

3   Does my boss really not understand the opportunities I can see? Perhaps it's time to prove them wrong and step out on your own.

4    Is my job making me ill? Life really is too short to spend doing something you don't enjoy. Understand what specifically is depressing you first though; starting a business can be a challenge too.

5    Am I breaching my employment contract? You've been trading on the side and are getting busier. Congratulations, you're already succeeding – but make sure that you're not breaching your employment contract.

## Going part-time helps you test the water

It's all too easy to decide that work is the cause of your unhappiness and that all will be well if you start out on your own. As with almost everything in life though, you can reduce the risk and dip your toe in the water by going part-time at work. This gives you time to try out your business idea without cutting yourself off completely from the security of regular income. Here are some factors to consider.

| Full-time | Part-time |
|---|---|
| You can grow faster | You'll grow more slowly |
| You need to make money sooner | You keep a salary as the business builds |
| More stressful, it feels 'all or nothing' | Also stressful, juggling too many balls |
| You are always able to respond to customers | You have to fit customers around work |
| People will take you seriously | People may not take you seriously |

Of course, management gurus such as Charles Handy have long advocated the 'portfolio career', where you build a collection of earning activities that suit your skills, lifestyle and income aspirations. For some, therefore, starting a new business part-time, while perhaps going part-time at work, is the best way forward.

 example

### Simon Moulson, Trade Credit Solutions

Simon worked in the insurance industry but after being made redundant three times decided to take control. He knew the industry, had a good network and had a growing reputation. He also knew that however well he did as an employee, he would always be vulnerable to the varying fortunes of the company he worked for.

All he lacked was the capital to start his business. He started Trade Credit Solutions from home, working part-time as a postman to pay the bills for the first year. Now, seven years later, he has a strong business operating in a niche market. He knows that his destiny is now firmly in his own hands. He is in control.

## CHAPTER 2

# Goals

Making sure your enterprise
fits your ethos

# 10 ways to help your family share your dream

A small business can be more demanding than small children. It will dominate your life so it really does make sense to get the whole family involved. If nothing else, it will help them to understand just why you're finding running a business so demanding. Here are ten ways to help those you love to understand.

1   **Get your kids online** – let's face it, your children are probably better at finding stuff online than you are. Why not get them to research your idea?

2   **Mystery shopping** – once you've spotted who your rivals are, get your relatives to pose as potential customers. Then ask them how they think you need to be different.

3   **Visit the bank** – let your partner pay in the cheques. It's a good way to help them feel good about your business. It's also one less job for you to do!

4   **Insource** – when you start out, managing costs is perhaps as important as generating sales. Use family labour to carry out the tasks you will one day outsource – stuffing envelopes, packing consignments, and so on.

5   **Carry the phone** – if you're out of the (home) office a lot and your partner is at home with the kids, a portable phone will be useful for taking messages for you. Make sure the baby doesn't cry!

6   **Paint the walls** – starting a business is fun. Get the whole family to help you prepare your office, shop or workshop.

7   **Fill the vase** – if you're a man you'll probably overlook some of the things that a woman would remember. Ask your partner to be responsible for keeping some flowers on your desk – it'll brighten your day.

8   **Change the fuse** – alternatively, if you're a woman, however competent at DIY, your partner will probably welcome being invited to be your maintenance man.

9   **Book a break** – you're busy and working hard but you need to take time out every so often. Set some dates, discuss a budget and ask your partner to surprise you and book regular breaks – even an evening out can be enough.

10  **Buy the vision** – everyone close to you needs to appreciate your vision for the enterprise you're establishing. It will make the inevitable sacrifices seem worthwhile.

Many people will tell you that you should never start a business with family or close friends. This is because emotional ties can make it difficult to remain objective and, as many family firms have found, it's difficult to fire someone you live with! However, many of the most successful businesses are run by husband and wife, brother and sister, or long-term friends. You just have to make sure that you put the business need first, rather than simply creating a role for someone you love.

 **tip**

### How to protect your relationship if you work with family or friends

- Have a written partnership or shareholder agreement that defines the deal.
- Use written job descriptions to define roles and job boundaries.
- Avoid intimacy in the workplace.
- Don't show favour – treat everyone the same.
- If you work with your partner, don't discuss work at home – have a life outside work!

**brilliant** **example**

### Shadowstar, spellsbyshadowstar.co.uk

Shadowstar is an astrologer, psychic and medium. Since childhood she has seen things differently from other people. As you can imagine, this doesn't make her the easiest person to live with!

Her business, Spells by Shadowstar, the name by which her clients know her, provides hope to people facing challenge and distress. Quite simply, she coaches clients to offer them the support and advice they need to cast spells easily themselves. You may not believe in magic yourself, but for those who do the service Shadowstar provides delivers real comfort and value.

Shadowstar could not have started her business without the support and encouragement of her husband and children. 'People tend not to sit on the fence on the subject of spell casting,' she explained. 'It's so important to my work and wellbeing to have them there to share both the successes and the snubs.'

# 10 common self-doubts and how to conquer them

It's natural to worry. Starting a business is a big responsibility and you're very much on your own. Here are ten common self-doubts and how to overcome them.

1   **I'm not bright enough** – well, sometimes you can be too bright to succeed. Innocence and naivety can actually protect you from fear. It is possible to think too much!

2   **I'm not pushy enough** – do you like doing business with pushy people or do you prefer nice, reasonable people? Pushy people are often less successful than you might think.

3   **I'm not rich enough** – one of the best ways to watch your costs is to have no money to waste. Wealthy people can be careless with money – you probably can't afford to be.

4   **I'm not good at sums** – relax, spreadsheets and accounting software make the numbers easy to work out. Remember that success is as much about instinct as arithmetic.

5   **I can't spell** – literacy is great if you want to write books but is less important if your business communicates with customers verbally. Use document templates – there are some in Chapter 20.

6   **I'll fail** – maybe you will, but equally you won't make your first million if you don't try.

7   **Rivals will eat me alive** – in fact the opposite is usually the case. Increasingly, it's the small, flexible and focused businesses that do best. Things change fast and you need to be eager to adapt, not stick in your ways.

8   **I'm naturally pessimistic** – so, you won't make false assumptions and step into the dark without a torch, will you? A glance at the downside puts the upside in perspective – just be sure to see both.

9   **I don't take risks** – running a business is like crossing the road. You can jaywalk, wear dark clothing and risk getting squashed – or push the button and follow the green man when the traffic stops. There's almost always a choice.

10  **I know my failings** – we all know what we're bad at and we all underestimate the value of our strengths. No one is perfect and nor is any business. That's why there's room for you too. Focus on what you do well.

Self-confidence is the product of knowledge and experience. Rather like riding a bike, playing a musical instrument or even making love, the more you practise the better you'll get.

Try to be objective and see through the marketing hype that rivals might be spreading around. Every entrepreneur has doubts, second thoughts and fears – you're not alone.

## brilliant example

**Con Lynch, CFE Group, Co. Kerry**

Raised on a small family farm in rural Ireland, Con could so easily have stayed on the land. His mother encouraged him to study and he was one of the few from his village school to go on to university. This was followed by a commercial career with a supplier of equipment to animal feed mills.

After a few years he wondered if he had what it took to start on his own. In Dublin one day for a football match, he bought a business start-up book and read it from cover to cover. 'It helped me realise that rather than trying to change my employer's company, I should simply start my own.'

He resigned from his job and spent three months travelling to research his business idea. The business Con started filled the market gap he felt his employer was neglecting. He now has a successful company that trades throughout Europe. He chose to base the company a few miles from where he was raised.

Con now devotes much of his time to being a role model, helping today's generation of local youngsters raise their aspirations. Having succeeded himself, he now enjoys encouraging others to do the same.

## brilliant recap

Human nature is such that we are all very aware of our own weaknesses and the strengths of others. It's very easy to persuade yourself that you are in some way inferior to other people. What you have to remember is that others will see you far more positively than you see yourself. Recognise your strengths and grow your self-confidence.

# 10 ways to work out how big you want to grow

Size isn't everything. Starting or growing a business should be prompted by personal ambition and goals. Remember that your enterprise is there to deliver your vision and your vision alone. Here's how to work out how big your business needs to be to realise your dream.

1   **How do you want to spend your time?** – you need to enjoy work itself as well as the financial rewards it might deliver. Only by doing what you enjoy and believe in will you succeed.

2   **How rich do you want to be?** – consider how wealthy you want to become and why. Perhaps you aspire to more than just money.

3   **What would you do if you could afford to?** – perhaps you're a social entrepreneur, driven by how you can help others while also helping yourself. Focus on the difference you want to make.

4   **Is your family behind you?** – your business must fit with their plans too. Remember that your partner as well as you may have to make sacrifices. Make sure they're with you.

5   **What do you want for your kids?** – watch them sleeping. What do you want for their future? How will your business deliver it?

6   **Consider risk** – the bigger the business, the bigger the risks. We all handle risk differently. Don't put yourself under more risk pressure than you're going to find comfortable.

7   **What do you want to change in the world?** – think about the world issues you'd like to change. If you make a mint, maybe you could invest in changing the world!

8   **Think balance** – take a long walk and watch nature. It's a great way to put your new venture in perspective with the world. Remember that there's more to life than work.

9   **Get some business heroes** – read how some of your business heroes got started. What can their business journey teach you? What do you want to do that's the same?

10  **Have a plan** – it's so obvious I've put it last, just in case you forget! Your plan needs to define the milestones you'll pass as you grow your enterprise. Writing it down will help you know deep down whether or not it's really what you want to do.

Of course, as Douglas Adams said in *The Hitchhiker's Guide to the Galaxy*, the answer to the ultimate question is 42. For you and me it is probably a little more complex and you will find that the more you achieve then the higher your aspiration will become. This is the phenomenon defined by Maslow as the 'hierarchy of needs':

- physiological – food, water, sleep, sex;
- safety – freedom from physical harm;
- social – friendship, a feeling of belonging;
- ego – respect and status;
- self-actualisation – developing talents and realising potential.

Many experts now say there's a further step. That once you have achieved self-actualisation, you will derive more satisfaction from helping others do the same. This is what motivates philanthropists to give their wealth away. It also encourages successful entrepreneurs to mentor and support those still building their businesses.

## brilliant tip

Find someone who has already enjoyed success and invite them to mentor you. Don't ask for too much of their time; all you need is for them to believe in you and to share their top tips when you encounter challenges.

## brilliant example

**Andy Kent, Andy's Kars**

An almost fatal brain haemorrhage brought Andy Kent's career as a motor mechanic to an abrupt halt. He lost the use of his right limbs and spent months recovering from his illness.

Finding it difficult to get work as a disabled mechanic, he started his own garage business. Andy's Kars provides all the usual motor services such as routine servicing, repairs and MOT testing. What makes it different is that the workshops have been designed to be used by mechanics with disabilities.

He recruits others who, like himself, don't want to let a disability prevent them from doing what they love. Not surprisingly, the company specialises in repairs to Motability adapted vehicles. Andy is driven not to make money, but to make possible what others said could not be done!

# 10 questions to help you match your business to your lifestyle

Your enterprise must fit you as perfectly as a made to measure suit. Many people would say a business is like a second skin, inseparable in virtually every way. Here are ten questions to ask to make sure you develop a business to fit your lifestyle.

1   **Rich or poor?** – if your household income doubled, what would you do differently? For some people, sudden wealth erodes personal values and brings misery. How much more would make you happy?

2   **Indoors or outdoors?** – do you like fresh air? If so, pay someone else to do the office work and spend your time out and about doing something you enjoy.

3   **Home or away?** – travelling to far-flung destinations is an enjoyable part of business life for some people. Others prefer to sleep in their own bed every night. Do you want to travel, or can you find the business you need close to home?

4   **Head or hands?** – thinking suits some people, craftsmanship others. You must choose how your time will be spent. As a craft business grows, its founder often leaves the workshop for the office, but this need not be the case. You make the rules.

5   **Night or day?** – are you a lark or an owl? Few newsagents or bakers dislike early mornings and you won't find an early bird running a night club. Match your enterprise to your body's natural rhythms.

6   **Alone or in a crowd?** – gregarious people like to work with others, while other people are more reclusive. Both are achievable – which are you?

7   **Fast or slow?** – some businesspeople thrive on short deadlines, surprise orders and multitasking (for example, distribution). Others prefer a more sedate style of work where time to reflect and think is valued (for example, law).

8   **Dirty or clean?** – like little boys and puddles, some entrepreneurs love cleaning blocked drains or rendering abattoir waste. Others prefer to import and distribute scented candles and incense sticks from mystical places.

9   **Healthy or harmful?** – selling cigarettes, guns or booze gives some people a problem. Don't start a business doing something you cannot morally condone. You must remain true to your personal values.

10  **Fat or thin?** – believe it or not, even today some businesses strike most of their deals over large lunches and dinners. If you're a closet gourmet you will relish the opportunity to munch your way to success. If you're a weightwatcher this will be less attractive.

One of the major problems encountered by the founder of a growing business is that they get to spend less time doing enjoyable things and more time in the office. This usually kicks in when you need to employ more than five people to handle the workload. In a nutshell, you become a manager and strategist. Crossing this barrier is often too great a problem and many owner-managers (often subconsciously) keep their business small enough to enable them to do the things they enjoy. Business advisers sometimes scathingly refer to these as 'lifestyle businesses'. There's nothing wrong with running a lifestyle business – it's your life after all. If, however, you do want to grow there are ways in which you can structure your business so that you do not lose touch with the coalface.

 **example**

### Rosemary Firth, Gallery 12a

An art teacher in Doncaster for 15 years, Rosemary wanted to change her life to include more art and less form filling! In 2009 she bravely decided to give up teaching and open an art gallery. As she said, 'Doncaster is not the world's most cultural town,' but deep down she felt there was an opportunity to try to change that perception.

Rather than simply displaying art and waiting for people to buy, she runs a wide range of classes in her gallery. She has 'Drawing for Beginners', 'Life Drawing' and a 'Children's Art Club'. This brings people into the gallery and enables her to put her teaching experience to good use.

Rosemary currently earns less from her business than she did as a teacher. But as she said, 'I am so much happier now.' There really is more to business than money.

**CHAPTER 3**

# Do research

Easy ways to check your
business idea

# 10 quick and simple ways to measure potential

Researching a new business idea is great fun. You have that feeling you're breaking new ground; the potential can look limitless. However, few ideas are completely new and the potential for most will be limited in some way or other.

Researching your business idea thoroughly is really important. It helps you establish exactly what you might be able to achieve. Remember that there may well be a real opportunity to find and exploit niche opportunities that would be uneconomic for big firms. Here are ten ways to quickly measure potential.

1   **Cost of entry** – business is like mining: the nearer the coal is to the surface, the smaller the seam you can profitably extract. Is it economic to get equipped for your business?

2   **Market maturity** – would you start a business selling fax machines? I doubt it as they are yesterday's technology, largely superseded by email. Make sure you face a growing market.

3   **PEST** – this is an acronym for political, environmental, social and technological. How are changes in each of these areas going to influence your business potential?

4   **Money** – you need to be realistic about money. Discard the more costly ideas and focus on those that need your expertise and experience more than they need investment.

5   **What happens right now?** – consider what you will be displacing. For example, if you've formulated a new sports drink, what brand will it replace? How do they compare? Will people change?

6   **Demand** – you might not need a huge demand to satisfy your needs, but is there enough? Remember that some businesses do very well serving small, niche markets.

7   **Repeat purchase** – the best businesses are those that provide things people need again and again. It enables you to build a customer base that keeps coming back for more.

8   **What's your exit plan?** – although right now you're probably not thinking about selling, you should be! The more marketable your business becomes, the more your potential return.

9    **What's driving you?** – lots of people start a business to get even with a former employer. That can help you stay motivated; it can also cloud your objectivity.

10   **Is this really you?** – potential alone is not enough to keep you interested and happy. You have to want to do this, as well as know that there's a market there to exploit.

## brilliant example

**Alan Jenkinson, Waterfront Manufacturing Ltd**

Alan did not set out to become an entrepreneur. He had a successful commercial career in the corporate clothing industry. Then things changed at work and he found himself no longer wanted. At the resulting industrial tribunal, Alan won a settlement large enough to set up his own business. He decided to get even!

He knew the marketplace and many of the customers. Although motivated by a need to prove his worth, he also knew he had to do things differently from his former employer. He acquired premises and equipment and decided to offer customers a wider spread, from promotional right through to quality tailored clothing.

Success quickly followed because, once his anger subsided, Alan actually knew what to do. He found he rather enjoyed being his own boss. As he recruited staff of his own, he vowed never to treat them as badly as he felt he'd been treated himself when last employed.

## Revenge

Alan was fortunate in that, although initially driven into entrepreneurship by his desire to get even with his former boss, he actually did have the knowledge and skills to succeed. Many people are less well equipped for the enterprise journey and come to regret their decision to go it alone.

To make sure you are not being driven into enterprise purely by a desire to seek revenge if you do suddenly find yourself out of work, feeling angry and perhaps bitter, check that:

●   you would not do better to go and work for a competitor to your old firm;

●   you understand that starting a business and getting over a career trauma are different things that often need to be worked on separately;

●   there are not others in the same situation you could team up with to start a stronger business.

# 10 free ways to research your idea on the internet

There is almost too much information out there to sift through when planning to attack a new market or start a new venture. You need to be selective and focus on what's most important to you. Here are ten top research tips.

1   **Google** – everyone uses search engines and Google is the most popular. However, try the 'advanced search' facility, which enables you to use more search criteria to improve the quality of what comes back.

2   **Check rivals** – look at the sites of those you compete with. Register to receive their regular newsletter or RSS feed – let them tell you what they're up to!

3   **Search people** – research the people you want to do business with, or perhaps those who compete with you. Find out what they're involved with – read their blogs, read criticism and praise.

4   **Read minutes** – most public organisations publish meeting minutes on the web. This can give you valuable background information if you're tendering for public sector work.

5   **Learn search techniques** – there are some clever things you can do with '&' and other symbols to gain specific information. Some examples are listed on page 30.

6   **Ask the obvious** – if you want to know what a word means, type into the search engine the phrase 'xxxxx means' and you'll probably get a definition back.

7   **Twitter** – this micro-blogging website offers a lot of potential once you've mastered how it works. It has been described as a 'human search engine', so search and ask questions.

8   **Numbers count** – many people forget that search engines can search phone numbers and postcodes. Google your own work phone number – you may be surprised what is revealed!

9   **Go to university** – you'll be amazed at how much new knowledge you can harvest from a university's website. You can use Google Scholar to search your subject and identify academics researching in your field of business.

10  **Check out books** – the book reviews on sites such as Amazon often contain enough to inform you without having to buy the book.

## Internet search techniques

Few people go beyond simply typing a word or phrase into Google and hitting the return key. Search engines are very sophisticated computer programs that can respond to quite complex requests. The internet is a crowded place, so the better your search technique, the better the results you'll get.

Here are some techniques gleaned from a variety of sources that you will find useful. Copy this page and keep it by your computer.

- **Use the best word** – search using the words you think others are most likely to have used when writing about what you're looking for. You need to strike a balance between the generic (too common) and the esoteric (too specialist).
- **Inverted commas** – enclosing words in inverted commas asks the search engine to find those words in that order. So '80 gsm copier paper' will find suppliers of copier paper of that weight, whereas searching for 'copier paper', or worse 'paper', will deliver many unwanted results.
- **Boolean logic** – this is a techie phrase for something quite simple. It uses the words 'and', 'or' and 'not' to filter results and present you with what you want. For example:
  - *locksmith* and *Epping* will exclude locksmiths based elsewhere;
  - *new cars* and *Epping* not *Ford* will exclude Ford dealers but show you the rest;
  - *new cars* and *Epping* and *Ford* or *Vauxhall* will give you only dealers selling Ford or Vauxhall cars.

You can also use '1' or '&' for 'and', and '–' for 'not'.

- **Capitals** – search engines are not case sensitive so you don't need to worry about capitals or lower case letters.
- **Parts of words** – some search engines will automatically search for and include variations of the words you search for. An example is 'dietary', which will also return pages showing 'diet'.

# 10 good questions and where to ask them

Research is all about the questions you ask. Get them wrong and you will miss vital information. Get them right and you discover all you need to know. Here are ten questions many people forget to ask.

1   **Would I buy it?** – this is actually a question about your personal values. If you wouldn't buy what you're planning to sell, why should anyone else? So be sure that if you were in the market for what you do, you'd buy without hesitation.

2   **Would others buy it?** – obvious and simple, but so many try to guess what the customer would say. Ask some prospective customers and hear it straight from the horse's mouth.

3   **Who already does it?** – check trade and online directories to see who's already offering what you're planning to offer. How can you be different?

4   **Where is it done best?** – take a journey to see the largest, fastest, best players in the business sector you're exploring. Few people travel to research their new ideas, so what you find works elsewhere may work for you at home.

5   **Does no competitors mean no market?** – there is very little that's completely new. Usually it's best to let someone else do the pioneering stuff, and then you can do it better. Worry if you seem to be the first – there may be no market demand.

6   **Would you be my mystery shopper?** – ask some friends to pose as customers and contact your rivals. Their feedback will reveal a lot about your competition and help you make your business different.

7   **What do the experts think?** – every business has its experts. They might be academics, journalists or professionals who advise your customer group. Get their feedback and act on what they say.

8   **Why is nobody selling XYZ here?** – sometimes a business just won't work whoever tries to run it. Make sure, for example, that you're not about to follow in the footsteps of others who have tried the same thing locally and failed.

9   **Why have you no outlets here?** – ask your suppliers why no one in your area has distributed their product before. Get their marketing people researching your idea – they will benefit from your success too.

10  **Does this feel right to me?** – finally, listen to your inner voice or instinct. Does this business idea feel right? Make sure you're not simply trying to convince yourself.

It is as easy to do too much research as too little. The most successful entrepreneurs rely as much on instinct and hunch as they do on research. If it feels right, they do it anyway. Sometimes you have to take a risk and do what you feel is right.

Remember that many of the world's most widely used products and services were established on a hunch and took a while to gain acceptance:

I think there is a world market for maybe five computers.

*Thomas J Watson of IBM, 1943*

No one will need more than 637 kb of memory for a personal computer.

*Bill Gates, 1970s*

As an entrepreneur, you have to balance your instinct against what you hear from those around you. The key to success, or even survival, is to manage risk and minimise the impact of failure. If you try different strategies some will fail as surely as others will succeed. Rather like the professional gambler, you need only to risk what you can afford to lose.

## brilliant    example

### Sharon Fernandez, www.thebabybook.co.uk

Sharon was a health visitor, working with mothers and their children in Essex. Over 15 years she became increasingly aware of the need for information for new mums to be more readily accessible. 'I had neither the time, energy nor inclination to trawl the internet, papers and local magazines for what was available for new mums,' she said. 'I so wished that there was a little booklet available that had all I needed to know in it.'

She also realised that baby-related businesses must find it difficult to reach their customers and so she researched the idea of connecting the two groups by publishing an annual *Baby Book*.

Sharon did her reseach quite simply by:

● talking to new parents and other health visitors;
● talking to suppliers of baby products;
● looking for the gap left by the many baby magazines.

Her research suggested that there was an opportunity and she took the plunge. Now, just a few years later, she has increased publication from once to three times a year. She has also been shortlisted for a prestigious local business award.

# 10 ways to test your new idea

OK, so you've done your basic research and think there's an opportunity. Next you have to test your new idea before you invest too much time, effort and money. Here are ten good ways to get real feedback before you go further.

1  **Ask a friend** – this is yet another time when the honest view of a trusted friend can save you lots of wasted effort and money. Tell them to be blunt, honest and explain why.

2  **Ask a customer** – showing potential buyers mock-ups, prototypes, and so on is a great way to involve them in your development work. Show them alternatives and have them say why they prefer one over the other. Hopefully this will also get you some early orders.

3  **Blog** – or start a Facebook group. Tell the right people what you are thinking and ask them to comment. Don't give too many secrets away though!

4  **Seek editorial** – your new idea might be newsworthy. Getting your story published might well stimulate enquiries. The journalist will also have a view and may be able to make some introductions.

5  **Ask ad agencies** – marketing folk spend their whole lives thinking of ways to market new things. Invite three agencies to pitch for your project. Their questions, comments and ideas will shape your thinking. If one of them has some brilliant ideas, hire them.

6  **Conduct street surveys** – stopping people in the street and soliciting their views is a great way to test a consumer business idea. Seek permission before doing this in a private shopping mall. In general, people are happy to pause and share their opinions.

7  **Use focus groups** – facilitated focus groups can get people thinking about and discussing your idea. The group literally thinks of the answers you want. Some researchers have special rooms where the meeting can be recorded for transcription and later analysis.

8  **Look elsewhere** – there's not much that's new and your idea is probably being exploited elsewhere. Use the internet to find similar enterprises that you can examine.

9  **Read research** – academics somewhere are probably researching in your business area. Delve into some academic journals and read what's being said.

10  **Just do it** – sometimes your instinct will be right whatever your market testing tells you. If you decide to 'just do it' make sure you limit your risk.

Large organisations spend huge amounts of money researching new ideas and opportunities. They don't always get it right. The motor industry is a good example. Quite a few new car models are developed, manufactured and launched only to be cut from the range within a year or two. This is a costly way to test the market and one that the small business can rarely afford to adopt.

## brilliant example

**Ben Handford, www.nakedmarketing.co.uk**

Having worked for two design companies since graduating, Ben didn't like the way people in his sector tended to use jargon to confuse the client and inflate the invoice. He recognised that integrity and trust were just as important as creativity in building long-term client relationships.

He decided to start his own agency with graphic designer and good friend Dave. They called their business Naked Marketing because nothing was hidden from the client. Within a year, it was clear that people respected their openness and willingness to tell it like it was. They built a strong client list and found that most shared their values and ideals.

When the recession hit in 2008, many of Naked's competitors lost clients and some went out of business. Ben's clients, on the other hand, stayed with Naked Marketing, recognising that they were already getting a fair deal. This helped the company hold its own in the downturn and emerge ready to grow when the economy began to recover.

# 10 people who might do your research for free

You can spend too much time researching. Here are ten other people/ organisations you can encourage to do the hard work for you.

1   **Advertising rep** – find the journals that reach your market and ask their advertising people why they deliver value. They will usually provide you with statistics from their research, and may even tell you about your rivals' advertising success.

2   **List broker** – you can buy lists of just about every type of person, business or organisation. A broker will tell you how many prospects there are. You don't have to buy the list!

3   **Government** – you'd be amazed how much data is posted on the internet by government departments and agencies. Ring the helpline and sweet-talk someone into extracting the data for you.

4   **Students** – college and school staff need business studies projects. If your research involves a lot of legwork, use students' legs to cover the ground.

5   **Trade associations** – you may not have joined the trade body that represents the sector you're exploring, but ring the librarian or information officer and ask for a membership list. Their website may also contain many useful downloads that will help you.

6   **Quangos** – most quangos publish detailed strategies and reports that show why they are needed and what they seek to do. If a quango exists to support your audience, ask to be sent whatever is available.

7   **Suppliers** – if you are a distributor, potential suppliers will usually be more than happy to let you have market information. They will already have researched it.

8   **Customers** – if the customer wants you to do something new, suggest it will happen faster if they can find others who will also buy. It's cheaper then for everyone.

9   **Undergraduates** – most universities have a website that markets work opportunities to students. Often, you can recruit a student to do your research for little more than the minimum wage. Many welcome an alternative to serving fast food to make money.

10  **Volunteers** – charities use volunteers all the time for fund-raising and much more. Sometimes you can recruit volunteers, or perhaps people with special needs, to assemble and collate market surveys in exchange for an appropriate donation to their cause.

Sometimes, the answer is right under your nose and you do not need to look very far at all to find the researcher you need.

 **example**

### Colette

Passionate about crafts, Colette wanted to set up an internet business that would make it easier to sell her work, as well as the work of others. Being a wheelchair user, getting out to research her business was not easy. 'Everything takes much longer and I need specialist office equipment so I cannot easily work in libraries.'

Fortunately, her son needed to write a business plan as part of his advanced business studies course. Colette suggested her own business idea for this project and so her son did all the research and applied the techniques his course had taught him to prepare a plan that worked for them both. He passed his course and Colette started her business.

## Entrepreneurship and disability

It would have been easy for Colette to give up. Severe arthritis means that she really needs to work from home so that she can work when her condition allows and rest when necessary. She needed specialist seating and office furniture, together with an ergonomic computer keyboard and mouse. As her own employer, she was able to obtain a government grant of several thousand pounds to cover the cost of equipment. If you have a physical condition that makes starting or operating your business a real challenge, you may also qualify for help towards the cost of the things you need.

**CHAPTER 4**

# Write your plan

How to make a convincing
case

# 10 things every business plan should contain

Every enterprise should have a business plan. It should not be lengthy or filled with jargon. Focus instead on making it short, simple, specific and, above all else, realistic. Remember that an overambitious business plan may fool others, but fool yourself and you will pay a heavy price. Be realistic and make sure your business plan contains the following ten things.

1   **Vision** – capture in a sentence what it is that makes this business exciting and utterly irresistible to customers, suppliers and, most importantly, to you.

2   **Background** – describe the context, experience and opportunity that tells you this is a good idea. Why is this the right time? What's changing in the world and how will this benefit your new venture?

3   **Goals** – what are the specific short-, medium- and long-term goals by which you will measure your success? Make them memorable and simple, then you won't forget!

4   **People** – describe the people, their skills and experience, that will make this vision a reality.

5   **Products/services** – what are you going to sell? What is the market gap you plan to occupy? Is demand growing?

6   **Competition** – who's already out there and how will you be different? Remember that people will buy what you do differently, not what you do the same.

7   **Marketing** – how are you going to find your customers and tell them the benefits they will gain from buying your products or services? How will you measure the response and so improve your marketing efficiency?

8   **Money** – how much do you need? Where will you find it? What's in it for your investors?

9   **Risk** – show that you've assessed the risks to your success and have them covered.

10  **Jumping ship** – a business, like anything else, has a natural lifespan. You need to plan for your exit before you start. Will you sell? Give it to your kids? What?

It is no coincidence that this checklist is one of the shortest in the book. The biggest mistake people make when writing a business plan is to make it too long. If you have a strong business case, it will be easy to explain and quantify.

 **tip**

Good business plans should be:

- **concise** – to the point and focused;
- **emotional** – you want to do this like it hurts, so tell the reader why;
- **logical** – giving you and anyone reading it confidence;
- **factual** – demonstrating your understanding of the opportunity;
- **realistic** – not committing yourself to too much.

Everyone who advises businesses will tell you that preparing a business plan is the essential first step. However, they will probably also tell you, if you ask them, that most business plans are filed in a drawer and never again looked at by those running the enterprise. The plan you write needs to be so relevant and useful that it becomes *part* of your business management. Here are a few myths about business plans.

- **I know my business and only need a plan to keep the bank happy** – sharing a simple, concise business plan with key employees is one of the best ways to keep their efforts aligned with your vision. Business plans are for you, not the bank.
- **Banks need lots of detail to show that I've considered all possible eventualities** – bank managers are people first and financiers second. The decision to lend will be made intuitively, with the manager's gut feeling for your business backed up by the plan you write. Yes, show you've considered the options, but keep it short too.
- **I've downloaded a great business plan model from the internet** – the internet is full of business plan frameworks into which you can drop your business. However, it's often best to copy the headings and write your own plan, using only those headings that are relevant and ignoring those that are not.
- **A consultant wrote my plan and the bank lent me £50,000** – sometimes, consultants and accountants are the best people to write your pitch to a funder. However, their starting point should be a business plan that you have written. No one else can really get into your mind and put your passion into the plan.

 **recap**

Your business plan is your route map. It describes your destination, why you're going and how you will get there. It should explain things as you see them, not as you think others expect to see them. Make it personal; make it yours!

# 10 important figures and how to calculate them

If you're new to business, or simply new to the numbers, the words people use when describing business plans can be confusing. Here are the ten figures you need to know best, together with how to work them out.

1  **Overheads** – the fixed costs of operating your business. It's the annual total of all the things you need to have, even if you sell nothing – for example, premises, equipment and staff.

2  **Variable costs** – incurred only when you produce something – for example, raw materials and transport. These costs are good because you incur them only when you've sold something.

3  **Profit** – as a rule of thumb, profit is the value of your sale less the associated variable costs less a proportion of your overhead costs. The more you sell, the more thinly your overhead costs are spread and the more profitable you become.

4  **Debtor days** – the average length of time customers make you wait for your money. Divide what you are owed today by your annual sales to arrive at how many days on average your customers take to pay.

5  **VAT** – if your sales rise above a certain annual level you have to register for value added tax (VAT). This means you have to add VAT to the sales price of most things, but you can also reclaim it on your business purchases.

6  **Creditor days** – the average length of time you string your suppliers along before paying your bills. Smart operators always pay the most important dependent suppliers first.

7  **Credit rating** – if you habitually pay your bills late and have perhaps had the odd court judgment made against your business, then your credit rating will be poor and people may ask for cash up front. Specialist agencies provide credit rating reports for a fee.

8  **Quick ratio** – this is the easiest accounting ratio to watch and also the most important. It is the total of the debt owed you plus the cash in your bank, divided by the amount you owe creditors. So, if your debtors (customers) owe you £10,000 and your bank account stands at −£2000, and you owe creditors (suppliers) £4000, your quick ratio is (£10,000 − £2000)/£4000 = 2. Above 1 and you are solvent, below 1 and you are not!

9    **Cash flow** – use a spreadsheet to calculate why you need your income to be phased to meet your predicted outgoings. Calculate the effect of people paying you late – it's alarming!

10   **Balance sheet and profit & loss** – these are reports that your accounting software will produce. Always look at the year-to-date figure as well as the last month's performance. You can rarely judge success on the strength of one month alone.

## Figures people

The good news is that you do not have to do all the work yourself. Accounting software takes much of the hard work out of bookkeeping and there are people who specialise in keeping books for others. Five reasons for using a good bookkeeper are:

- someone else is checking your figures;
- invoicing is not delayed because you are too busy;
- they save you time and hassle;
- accountant's bills are lower if a bookkeeper has done the basics;
- you have someone else who can chase overdue payments.

### brilliant  example

**Kathrine Overton, Overton Cleaver LLP, www.overtoncleaver.co.uk**

Kathrine started a bookkeeping business at home. It enabled her to work and look after her young family. As the children grew, so did the business, but she remained home based. Some clients needed regular time spent at their offices, so Kathrine found associates able to work on her behalf on her clients' premises.

Later, she found a need for training in Sage Accounting software. Many of her clients were using Sage and she realised that helping them become more confident using the software would help her clients do more for themselves. It also meant she could focus on the work she enjoyed best – Sage training.

Finally, in 2008 Kathrine teamed up with lifelong friend Maxine Cleaver, also an accountancy professional. Together they provide a comprehensive, hands-on accountancy and bookkeeping service to a growing client list. The business remains based at Kathrine's home.

## brilliant tip

If your business sells to the public (who cannot reclaim any VAT you add), you might be better to keep your turnover under the VAT registration threshold. You can then charge less than your VAT registered competitors and still make more profit.

# 10 things your bank managers like to see

Even if you don't need to borrow money, it's good to act as if you do. It has often been said that pitching your business plan to a bank is a very useful reality check. It also means that you are starting a banking relationship that will become increasingly important as your enterprise grows. Bank managers see a lot of entrepreneurs and read many business plans. Here are ten words you should make sure are included in your business plan. Each will impress.

1   **Vision** – you must show that you have a clear vision and know just where you are heading. Your plan must paint a clear picture of your vision. Make it exciting!

2   **Commitment** – show how you are making a big commitment to the business yourself. Bankers like to see you risking more of your own money than you do of theirs.

3   **Security** – as if commitment is not enough, banks usually want guarantees. This often means giving them a legal charge over your home or other assets. If this makes you feel uncomfortable ask yourself why.

4   **Risk** – how big is the risk you're taking? Show that you've looked at some different scenarios. Also show how your past experience minimises the risk.

5   **Market** – it helps if your banker understands your market. In really specialist sectors, it is often best to seek out bankers familiar with your sector.

6   **Skills** – your CV, and those of your key people, must read well. No bank will lend if your motive for starting is that you were sacked for failing in someone else's business.

7   **Health** – you need resilience and stamina. Invest in a medical check-up and add the report to your plan.

8   **Love** – the clever banker visits you at home to assess how committed your family is. Remember, it's often their home you're risking.

9   **Guts** – if you're too soft you won't chase your debts and might fall behind with loan repayments. You need to come over as tough, but not macho!

10  **Persuasiveness** – the ability to sell is the greatest asset in any entrepreneur. Don't appear too glib or too clever. Practise selling on the bank. You don't have to take all that's offered to you!

## More stuff about banks

Everybody likes to knock banks, particularly after the 2008–10 recession. The fact is though that every business needs the services of a bank and, managed correctly, banks are an asset and not a threat to your success. Online banking is very convenient and gives you the comfort of being able to check at any time of the day or night that your customers have paid.

Banks are, however, a supplier to your business like any other and you should never be afraid to consider changing to another. Here's a checklist to help you decide whether or not your bank is giving you good service. Check out alternative banks if:

- you find it difficult to get on with your bank manager;
- the charge over your home is not released when your business becomes a lower risk;
- good quality online banking is not available;
- every meeting turns into a sales pitch for overpriced insurance products;
- your bank does not really understand your industry.

Here are some other things to consider.

- You can make it easier to deal with your bank if you:
  - tell your bank manager (almost) everything and don't hold back information;
  - invite your bank manager to visit your business for a first-hand inspection;
  - discuss business over lunch or even in a convenient coffee house;
  - take a genuine interest in your bank manager as a person;
  - thank the bank for doing well, in addition to moaning when it goes wrong.
- Cash transactions – surprisingly, some banks do not like handling large amounts of coinage. Some work through the Post Office network and do not charge to take cash deposits.

● Credit cards – shop around before accepting your usual bank's 'merchant services' offer if you want to take credit cards. This is especially true if you plan to take online payments where there are specialist service providers.

 **brilliant** recap

Everyone likes to complain about bank managers. The fact is that when they say no to a business plan, it's often because it's not a very convincing plan!

# 10 shortcuts to an accurate cash flow forecast

Your business plan will inevitably contain forecasts and predictions. Certainly in the early days, cash flow forecasting is the most important factor as it will chart the journey to profit. Checking your financial progress is vital if you are to stay on track. Don't underestimate the following ten aspects of your enterprise's financial health.

1   **Cash** – always aim to borrow or invest more than the forecast says you need. This will allow for slippages later. It's what your overdraft facility is for.

2   **Sales** – building up sales, be it a new business or a new product, always takes longer than you think. Be modest in the estimate for your early months.

3   **Purchases** – if you are to carry stock or use raw materials, it will take a while to reach the right usage levels. Allow for overstocking at first.

4   **VAT** – many people forget to add VAT to purchases and sales, and to allow for the quarterly tax payment. VAT can both underpin and wreck cash flow!

5   **Employment costs** – as well as adding a percentage for National Insurance payments, you need to allow for staff training, temps for sickness cover and any equipment your staff will need. Use a payroll bureau to calculate your true employment costs.

6   **Paying the tax man** – make sure you build in your tax and VAT payments. They can be large figures so these payments need to be planned.

7   **Marketing costs** – you will waste much of your marketing budget on experimenting. If sales are slow you may want to spend even more. Build 'more' into the forecast.

8   **Include options** – the above are all largely pessimistic points. Duplicate your forecast and add in some optimistic predictions. See how these make a huge impact on your need for cash. Now plan how to make some of those good things happen.

9   **Loan repayments** – at some point, you'll want your investment back, with interest. If it's the bank's money this will be prescribed. Include repayments in your forecast.

10  **Slippage** – work out what effect late payment by your customers will have on your cash requirement. Frightening, isn't it?

## Microsoft Excel

Chances are you're pretty good at putting together spreadsheets. Just in case you're not, here are some top tips for MS Excel.

- A useful spreadsheet for calculating loan rates can be found under *General Templates > Spreadsheet Solutions > Loan Amortization.*
- Use the *Ctrl* and *:* keys together to enter the current date into a cell.
- Experiment with *Tools > Goal Seek*, especially with cash flow forecasts. This can help in achieving desired profits by changing product/service rates.
- Remember that Excel has built-in database functionality. With long lists of data, try using *Data > Filter > AutoFilter* to add filtering options.
- Don't forget the S button on the standard toolbar. This can be used to sum ranges easily. Also, hidden in the dropdown menu are *Min*, *Max* and *Average* functions.

**brilliant** example

**Duane Jackson, Kashflow, www.kashflow.co.uk**

Duane started his first business with help from The Prince's Trust. He looked for software to help him manage his accounts. What he found seemed to be more geared towards making life easy for the accountant than for the business owner. He decided to develop an online, integrated bookkeeping package that focused on the needs of the business owner.

These days, his business is a market leader with thousands of satisfied users. As his business grew, so he recruited the experts he needed to keep his product developing. Despite now employing many with an accounting background, he has stuck with his simple ethos: make it easy for the business owner to use and afford and everything else then becomes easy!

# 10 points to consider when choosing a business structure

Your accountant will probably advise you to structure your business solely to reduce tax. However, there are other equally important things to take into account. Here are ten of them.

1  **Risk** – if your business operates in fields where financial risks are high, it will be better to protect yourself by setting up a limited liability company. This limits your personal liability, unless you can be proved to have acted wrongfully.

2  **Reward** – how much money do you expect, or want, to make? If your business is going to remain modest, it may be better to be self-employed or in a partnership.

3  **People** – shared ownership of a business can be very tax efficient. Equally, giving shares to people not involved from day to day (for example, your family) can be a problem if the relationship sours. Sometimes it's best to own the business outright and pay more tax!

4  **For sale?** – limited companies, whose accounting is reported to Companies House, are easier to sell because trading is more transparent.

5  **Socially motivated?** – if you are establishing a UK social enterprise, you might set up as a community interest company. This gives you the flexibility of a limited company and the transparency of purpose of a charity (see **www.cicregulator.gov.uk**).

6  **Don't divorce** – not a pleasant thought, but if you put half of your business in your partner's name to save tax you'll have a problem if you separate.

7  **Selling up** – the tax treatment of the proceeds from the sale of business shares and assets often makes creating a company a good move. Take advice before you start.

8  **Customer perception** – in some marketplaces you are not taken seriously unless you have a limited company. This is perhaps rather silly but true all the same. You must decide whether you are going to make a stand or follow the herd.

9  **Trading name** – even if you decide not to set up a limited company you can still use a memorable trading name. If the name you want is not registrable, you may still be able to be ABC Ltd, trading as Alphabets. One is the business and the other the brand.

10  **Reputation** – just to remind you that what you do, and how others see your business, is actually more important than how you set the business up!

Some people go to extraordinary lengths to make their business appear to be something it isn't. This often has as much to do with their feelings of insecurity as any practical need. Here are some ways to make your business look real.

- **You** – in most small businesses, like it or not, you are the business. How you behave, and indeed your level of confidence, will say most about the firm.
- **Phone 1** – answering the phone professionally, without background noises
  from children, the TV or your pet parrot, suggests you are in an office and focused on work.
- **Phone 2** – if you work from home, invest in a separate business line. It's possible to forward calls and much more. Explore the options.
- **Email** – domain names are so cheap now that there really is no excuse for being yourco@hotmail.com. Buy your domain and look businesslike.
- **Address** – as long as you make sure that you use your postcode and talk nicely to your postman, you can drop '147 Station Road' and replace it with YourCo, Station Road.

## brilliant example

### Richard Osbourne, Blue Pearl Photographic

A talented graphic designer and photographer, Richard couldn't afford to rent business premises when he started his business, preferring instead to invest in a top-of-the-range Apple Mac computer. He lived in a flat in a nice part of the city and decided to change his address to 'Studio 5, 123 The Street'. By calling his flat a studio and meeting his clients at their office, or in a convenient coffee shop, he saved money he would have spent in rent. He was also able to work when it suited him without having to leave home.

When his business had grown enough to employ an assistant, he did a deal with a client, moving into an empty office at their workplace and offsetting their work against the rent. This way, he also secured the long-term support of a key client.

## CHAPTER 5

# Get advice

Find people able to help you

# 10 people who can offer you the best advice

You will find many people only too willing to offer you their opinion. But what you really need is advice from people with relevant knowledge and experience. Opinion is important and can help you shape your view. Good advice is more valuable, steering you away from potential pitfalls. Here are ten different people who can advise you.

1   **Parents** – they probably know you better than they know your business. Parents can help you be realistic and work within your personal and emotional capabilities.

2   **Bank manager** – like you, your bank manager wants to see your enterprise grow and comfortably service its debts. Listen to their advice; they've usually seen it all before.

3   **Accountant** – your accountant will always see more risks than opportunities. Let them keep your feet on the ground.

4   **Independent financial advisers** – if your business needs to borrow or invest, a good IFA will usually offer more options than a bank. Make sure though that you talk to someone familiar with people like you, with high aspirations and goals.

5   **Consultants** – always judge a consultant by their track record. Experience and testimonials are more important than qualifications. Be wary of those who claim to be able to save you money – they will cost you money first!

6   **Friends** – rather like parents, friends know you better than they know your business. Encourage them to use their networks to introduce you to new customers.

7   **Customers** – always listen to your customers. Their feedback can be invaluable as you strive to develop your business. Invite constructive criticism and act on it.

8   **Suppliers** – invite your most important suppliers to offer their advice. Not only can they help you get more value from their products or services, but they also understand your business sector.

9   **Support agencies** – there's a whole world of government-funded business advice out there. Much of it is good and almost all of it is unbiased and sincere.

10  **Yourself** – yes, you are probably your own best-qualified business adviser. Listen to your intuition and take time to reflect on what that inner voice tells you.

## Action learning groups

Many people find it difficult to act on good advice. Usually it means doing something differently and often work gets in the way. As your own boss, you have no one to tell you to follow advice and so drifting along is all too easy.

Most business communities have one or more action learning group. These have different names and are often linked with a university or college. Business support agencies sometimes set them up too. 'Action learning' is a proven way of helping busy entrepreneurs develop their businesses.

If you join an action learning set, you will find:

- a group of like-minded fellow entrepreneurs;
- regular meetings at which you openly and confidentially discuss business issues;
- an experienced facilitator, often from a business school;
- pressure from your peer group to put into action the changes you discuss and agree with the group.

In short, action learning makes you accountable and makes you hold others accountable too. It's a very effective way to develop your business. It's also very good to have a bunch of like-minded business owners in whom you can confide. You will find yourself able to help others as well, however inexperienced you feel when you join.

 **tip**

The best advice always comes from people who have faced the same issue.

# 10 things to check when choosing a business adviser

Business advisers come in all shapes and sizes. What's important is that they can quickly relate to what you're trying to do and are clearly able to help. Whoever you choose to share your business challenges with, make sure they have all or some of the following characteristics.

1  **Empathy** – check that they are on your wavelength as a human being. We're all different and you have to feel comfortable that you and your adviser understand each other as people.

2  **Knowledge** – they should be familiar with your business sector and with organisations your size. Ideally they'll have recent experience of doing what it is you're trying to do right now.

3  **Interest** – they need to be interested in your challenge, and not just because they might profit from it. Your adviser must believe in what you are trying to do, otherwise why would they help?

4  **Enthusiasm** – check that they have enthusiasm and a willingness to explore new ideas with you rather than recycle old ones. Pick someone with spark and a passion for pushing back boundaries.

5  **Contacts** – check that they have contacts with other people able to help you make it happen. You want people who 'know who' as well as 'know how'. Both are vital to your success.

6  **Open mind** – you must work with someone who will listen and is prepared to be challenged. Ideally, they'll learn as much from you as you do from them.

7  **Track record** – it's not enough to talk about it, you want someone who's been there several times and bears the scars. Ask for testimonials and case studies.

8  **Ethics** – this will ensure that you won't be led to places you find uncomfortable. We all have different moral standards, so choose someone who shares yours.

9  **Wealth** – the best advisers are those who don't need your project to pay the bills.

10  **Radar** – this is the ability to see what's just over your business horizon.

 **recap**

There are two kinds of business adviser – those you pay and those paid by someone else, usually ultimately by the government. You're more likely to take seriously someone you've paid for with your own money.

## Brief

It's always a good discipline to write down what you want a consultant to give you. A written brief means you both know what is expected. It also means you can ask more than one to pitch for the work in a way that will make comparison easier. When preparing a brief for your adviser, remember to include:

- an overview of what your business does;
- your vision for the future;
- the key issues you feel you are facing;
- how you feel an adviser can help;
- your budget and what you expect to see from your investment.

**brilliant** **example**

**Norfolk Knowledge, www.norfolkknowledge.co.uk**

Norfolk Knowledge links the wealth of experience within the community with people in need of some free help and advice. It was set up by Norwich Business School and is supported by Norfolk County Council.

It provides opportunities for those retired or working on a portfolio basis to share their experience with people starting out or facing particular challenges. The volunteers are all people who have succeeded in their respective fields and want to contribute to the success of the next generation.

Your local business school might have set up a similar network. Why not look and see?

# 10 ways to find a mentor and why it's important

Most really successful people have a mentor. A mentor is someone who takes a genuine interest in supporting your success. Whereas an adviser will focus on your business, a mentor will focus on you. Here are ten top tips in relation to business mentors.

1 **Aim high** – the best mentor you can get is someone 20 years older than you who is highly successful in your field. Don't work with someone comfortable achieving second best.

2 **Be bold** – it's easy to rule out your best potential mentor by assuming they'll say no. In reality though, those rarely asked are often flattered and sometimes say yes!

3 **Just ask** – there is no secret to recruiting a mentor. You just have to find the right person, research them to find the common interests and pop the question.

4 **Why me?** – this is what the best potential mentors ask. You need to have three good reasons that will encourage them reluctantly to say yes.

5 **Be realistic** – it's usually better to meet a really good mentor once a quarter than a poor mentor once a week. The best people have little spare time but will be surprisingly perceptive.

6 **Be challenged** – a good mentor will gently stretch your comfort zone and be there to support you when you wobble.

7 **Get connected** – a mentor who knows your marketplace will be able to open doors for you too. This should never be their main role, but it does help justify the cost.

8 **Agree goals** – work out what you both want from the relationship and agree some measurable goals. Report monthly on progress, even if you do not meet.

9 **Help your mentor** – there may be ways you can help your mentor achieve their goals too. Don't assume though, simply ask.

10 **Follow through** – there's nothing more irritating for a mentor than someone you're mentoring not delivering what they've promised. If you get a mentor, you must do everything you say you'll do.

## Examples of good mentoring

Good mentoring is like good parenting. The mentor gives time and expertise quite simply because they want you to grow and develop. Mentoring can take several forms. Here are some good examples.

- **The Prince's Trust** – this charity recruits volunteer mentors to support vulnerable youngsters starting a business. The mentors have business experience and are happy to help someone else get their enterprise off the ground. The organisation trains its mentors and provides a monthly reporting system so people know what to expect.
- **Senior managers** – people nearing the end of their careers often mentor younger managers in their own organisation. This helps grow the next generation of leaders.
- **High fliers** – large organisations often encourage their high fliers to mentor people in other sectors, usually the voluntary sector. This widens their experience and develops their leadership qualities.
- **Industry 'godfathers'** – you know who they are. Former pioneers now winding down at the end of a tumultuous career. They can sometimes be encouraged to mentor those at the lower end of the ladder they've climbed.

 **brilliant**    **recap**

An adviser can tell you what you should do and a mentor supports you as you do it.

# 10 things advisers can always do better than you

However hard you try, it's really difficult to remain objective when you are so close to the coalface. A good adviser can help you see and deal with the barriers that every entrepreneur encounters. Here are ten examples.

1   **Marketing** – seeing your business through your customers' eyes will always be easier for someone other than you. Marketing advisers will often have experience of what works best in your business sector.

2   **Innovation** – doing old things in new ways, or simply doing new things, requires you to stop long enough to think. Consultants give you the time, and they have been there before.

3   **Cost control** – a fresh pair of eyes can often see more than you clearly where profits are leaking from your company.

4   **Funding** – finding the money to grow needs a combination of accountancy skills and a good knowledge of the finance field. What's more, the right adviser will already have a reputation with lenders. A plan that they help you write may carry more weight.

5   **Hiring** – it is nearly always best to let someone else help you recruit. Even if you'd prefer not to use an agency, have someone independent interview alongside you.

6   **Training** – balancing your business needs with the skills available, and planning how to plug the gaps, is crucial. Why not get an expert to help?

7   **Firing** – it may seem a cop-out, but if you've got a problem member of staff then a specialist in employment law can help to sort it out. There's lots of tricky legislation to consider.

8   **IT** – technology is constantly changing. Make sure someone is keeping you up to date.

9   **Property** – whether buying, selling, building, altering or adapting, most people get outside help with sorting out property issues.

10  **Introductions** – the best advisers have a good network of contacts. Why not get yourself plugged into someone else's network?

## Consultants

While many business advisers are government funded, consultants rarely work for free. Consultants are like cars – they come in all shapes and sizes and there's usually a choice within your price range. As with cars, it's no good buying a cheap one if you want to make a long journey. Equally, the top-of-the-range model might be good for your ego, but if you simply want to potter around the block it's a bit of a waste. Here are some places you might look to find a consultant.

- **Ask a friend** – they may be able to recommend someone they've been happy with.
- **Support agencies** – they have lists of vetted consultants who they know can do the job.
- **Accountants** – they usually know who can deliver and who to avoid.
- **Business networks** – most business networks are full of consultants; it's where they go to meet new clients. Ask them for past clients you can talk to. Testimonials are everything!
- **Professional bodies** – these often have experts in the field you are exploring.

Consultants tend to come in two types – strategists and tacticians. Here's how to choose between them.

| Strategists | Tacticians |
| --- | --- |
| Help you decide where to go | Grab your hand and take you there |
| Write well-researched reports | Write realistic operational plans |
| Are often academically gifted | Often have battle scars |
| Rarely want to get involved in delivery | Usually work best on a specific issue |

## CHAPTER 6

# Find the cash

How to fund start-up and growth

# 10 places to look first to finance your business

Asking a bank for money is always a good starting point. They will check out your proposal for free and give you valuable feedback. However, the bank might not be your only option. Here are ten places you might look to when trying to find money for your business.

1   **Your savings** – it really is important that if you can afford to invest in your business that you do. Only when your own money is involved will you take your enterprise seriously.

2   **Your mortgage lender** – increasing the mortgage on the family home is the traditional and cheapest way to raise business capital. Your partner must agree if the home is jointly owned.

3   **Parents** – be honest with them. You are probably a beneficiary of their will so all you are actually asking for is an advance. Check for tax benefits that might help you both.

4   **Siblings** – brothers and sisters who are successful in their lives might be happy to invest in your success. So too might other family members. Don't take advantage of family though.

5   **Your boss** – can you negotiate a voluntary redundancy package? Alternatively, see if the firm will lend you the money; former employers frequently become first customers.

6   **Your life partner** – does your life partner love you enough to lend you the cash? Would their family invest in your venture? Perhaps you are both involved in the start-up anyway.

7   **Friends** – people who believe in you might be prepared to invest in your business. Several could club together to help you. They might also accept variable repayments linked to how well you're doing.

8   **A man in the pub** – never underestimate those you know but know little about. The man you drink with might well be a willing investor.

9   **Suppliers** – people who will benefit from your venture may not put in cash but might well lend you equipment or be happy to give you extended credit.

10  **Customers** – your early customers may be happy to invest in the business and then take their return as discounted products or services. This happens more often than you might think!

Dr Hermann Hauser, founder of Acorn Computers and now a venture capitalist in Cambridge, says that the first port of call for anyone looking for additional funding should be 'family and fools'. What he means is that those who have faith in you will be the most likely to invest. Those with money and little common sense should also not be discounted. It is a matter for you and your conscience how far down the 'fools' route you decide to go.

## brilliant example

**Jo Behari, Home Jane, www.home-jane.co.uk**

Jo was bored with her job and so four years ago set up Home Jane. The company supplies female tradespeople all over London and the South East. Jo loved DIY and knew that some women found male tradespeople intimidating. She had spotted her opportunity to meet a need and do what she enjoyed. 'I didn't feel comfortable committing to external finance,' she says, 'so I raised the £5000 I needed by remortgaging my flat.' Jo felt more comfortable being in control like this, and so for her it was the right thing to do.

Now she has a thriving, profitable business with more than 50 tradeswomen on her books. She spends more time in the office than with her power tools but loves every minute of her day.

# 10 less obvious places to look for funding

The list you've just read contains all the obvious places people look for business funding. It is surprisingly common for people to borrow from family, friends and acquaintances. You might not be comfortable with that, so here are some alternatives.

1   **Local government** – in many communities there are business loan schemes to help people get started. They're more often found where there are high levels of unemployment or disadvantage. Do some checking.

2   **The Prince's Trust** – this charity makes business loans and sometimes gives grants. To qualify you must be aged under 30 and be unable to borrow elsewhere. Ask any business adviser to introduce you.

3   **Credit cards** – quite a few people have funded their business with credit cards. Interest rates charged are punitively high. Consider credit cards only as a last resort.

4   **Credit unions** – these organisations are set up in disadvantaged communities to replace loan sharks. Although usually focused on consumer lending, many also make small business loans.

5   **Social lenders** – under a scheme called the 'community development finance initiative' (CDFI) there are specialist lenders that can offer their investors tax incentives. To qualify for this, the organisation has to lend to people considered at a disadvantage. (Almost anyone turned down by a bank can meet the criteria!)

6   **Insurance policies** – it's rarely a good idea to cash in an insurance policy. However, many will allow you to borrow from them at a low rate of interest. You are, after all, borrowing your own money in many respects.

7   **Your cash flow** – to put it simply, if your customers pay you before you pay your suppliers, you have positive cash flow and need to borrow less.

8   **Asset finance** – this is where you borrow against the value of business assets and equipment. It enables you effectively to sell and lease back capital items you wish with hindsight you'd financed differently.

9   **Factoring** – this and invoice finance both loosely describe the same thing. A bank agrees to pay you say 80 per cent of the invoice value when it is issued. They then collect payment from your customers and return the balance to you after fees and interest have been deducted.

10 **Charity grants** – if your enterprise is focused on social good as much as or more than it is on profit, you may qualify for a grant. This is particularly true if your business is structured as a social enterprise.

 **tip**

Whenever you borrow money for your business you will have to pay it back. Only borrow what you are confident you can repay.

**brilliant    example**

**Catherine Carter, www.catherinecarterphotography.co.uk**

Catherine had a young family when she started her business and money was tight. She had run a hairdressing salon from home for a while but knew that photography was her real passion.

To set herself up she needed a decent car, equipment and displays to take to wedding shows. She funded these with credit cards, paying off the loans as soon as work started to come in.

Now she wins most of her work by recommendation. She freely admits that borrowing on credit cards was a gamble, but one that in her case quickly paid off.

# 10 ways to reduce the amount you need, maybe to zero!

At first glance, most businesses need a lot of money to set up and grow. However, with a little more thought and creativity, sometimes you can start or grow a business without increasing your borrowing. Here are ten ways to make sure you need to borrow less.

1   **Share stuff** – you probably have many things on your list for investment that you don't need to own at all. Sharing stuff with business neighbours, suppliers and customers can save cash.

2   **Squat!** – empty premises quickly deteriorate. Landlords will sometimes let people occupy business premises for free (or almost for free) in exchange for paying the rates and keeping the place safe.

3   **Use agency staff** – if your business needs people in varying amounts, use agency staff. These will cost a little more per hour, but are only costing you when you need them.

4   **Subcontract** – it's natural to want to do everything yourself. However, as you grow, it usually makes sense to specialise in what you do best and contract out other tasks.

5   **Be frugal** – remember that old adage and look after the pennies. Lots of small costs can soon add up. Only spend on what is really necessary.

6   **Read contracts** – small print is small for a reason; people want you to gloss over it without reading the detail. Always check what you're signing up to and avoid costly surprises.

7   **Sell scrap** – in some businesses disposing of waste is a large expense. Sometimes you can find someone able to use and pay for your waste – for example, firewood from a furniture factory.

8   **Buy scrap** – equally, you might be able to buy and make use of other people's waste. A brilliant example is the fishing rod mail order company that posts customer orders out in the cardboard tubes a carpet retailer had to dispose of when a roll was finished.

9   **Bid on auction websites** – you can dramatically reduce the investment you need for almost anything by buying it through websites like eBay.

10  **Be creative** – there are two ways to do everything. Before accepting and investing in the obvious, look for alternatives.

## Good examples of creative set-up cost saving

A graphic designer rents a desk in an existing design studio. They find they can:

- share equipment rather than buy their own;
- pick up overflow work from their landlord and actually earn their rent;
- benefit from being part of a creative community rather than on their own.

Three organic farmers set up a shared warehouse and buy a van together. They find that:

- they each specialise in producing different things, reducing competition;
- the van delivers for them all, improving customer service and reducing costs;
- all run promotions offering their customers introductory deals on each others' produce.

A school teams up with a training provider. They find that:

- the trainer uses school resources in the evenings;
- the school offers training to parents and staff;
- the school office handles the trainer's bookings and admin at lower cost than hiring an assistant.

# 10 demands investors sometimes make

Everyone who invests in your business will want to see a return. Your mother may be content with the emotional payback, but others will be less generous. When negotiating finance you need to bear in mind the demands any investor is going to make. Here are some to look out for.

1 **Security** – this means that your lender wants to be able to recover their debt if you default on your loan. It is a generic term for guarantees, legal charges and debentures.

2 **Personal guarantee** – this is a simple legal contract that means you agree to repay the loan if your business cannot.

3 **Second charge** – this is like a second mortgage as it is usually secured against your home. It's like a personal guarantee but stronger as the lender knows the value is there.

4 **Debenture** – this is a legal charge over your unpaid customer invoices. It means that if the business fails, your lender has first call on the money your business is owed.

5 **Shares** – while 1–4 apply mostly to banks, other investors will want a share of the business. If you've seen *Dragons Den* on TV, you'll understand what this means.

6 **Buying restrictions** – some brewers lend money to pub landlords in exchange for being the only supplier of beer. Others businesses might do the same. Will you remain competitive with less freedom of choice?

7 **Pricing restrictions** – similarly to above, you might find yourself committed to supplying goods or services to your investor at less than market price.

8 **Dividends** – these are a proportion of your profits distributed to your shareholders. If you have an outside shareholder, they'll want a share of your profits.

9 **Profit share** – the formal investor in your limited company will expect dividends. Informal investors in you will often negotiate their own profit sharing agreement.

10 **Favours** – this covers everything else an investor might expect from you. Interpret it as you wish, but do not let an investor dominate your business or your life.

## Investor risk and return

Many small business investments are based on intuition. They may be quite informally negotiated and repaid. Others will be much more rigorously assessed and toughly negotiated, often with accountants and lawyers hired to advise both sides.

However large or small the investment, the basic rules remain unchanged:

● the greater the risk, the greater the interest rate of shareholding demanded;

● the lower the risk, the wider your options;

● the more you invest yourself, the better the deal you will negotiate;

● the newer your business, the greater the perceived investor risk;

● the better you keep records and accounts, the stronger the case you can argue.

 **brilliant** recap

Once you've given away a share of your business it is no longer all yours.

# 10 things about overdrafts you need to know

It is a myth that every business has to have an overdraft. It is true that few can manage growth without overdrafts, but those that do are often the best. When negotiating your overdraft, be aware of the following ten points.

1   **Guarantee** – overdrafts are nearly always underwritten by your personal guarantee. You're effectively paying a high interest rate to borrow your own money.

2   **Mortgage** – increasing your mortgage on your home can provide cheap money for your business. Your personal liability is no greater than if you had an overdraft.

3   **Fees** – banks charge fees to arrange overdrafts, take guarantees and anything else they can think of. These fees can be significant but are often negotiable.

4   **Not permanent** – overdrafts can be called in by your bank at any time. If worried about your business, banks often wait until your balance is positive and then withdraw the overdraft.

5   **More debt equals less profit** – remember that paying interest on loans is eating into your profit. Reduce your borrowings and your profits go up.

6   **It's your business** – remember that your bank is a supplier like any other. Don't let them call the shots – there is probably someone else who will be happy to step into their shoes.

7   **Reports** – most banks demand monthly management accounts when you're in the red. This is good practice, but do make sure you understand them before posting.

8   **Bouncing cheques** – one of the most damaging things any business can do is issue a cheque that bounces. It suggests that you're not managing your cash flow and leads to loss of trust.

9   **Cash flow forecasts** – before borrowing, work out when your cash flow will render the overdraft unnecessary. If it doesn't, there may be a problem with your costings.

10  **Insurance** – many banks sell you insurance so that the overdraft is repaid if you die or get very sick. This insurance can be surprisingly expensive – it's another one of those unexpected costs.

Of course, overdrafts are not all bad news and most of us have them from time to time. The art is not thinking of an overdraft as being essential, especially when you start your business. Too many people use their overdraft to pay themselves a salary when, frankly, they'd be better living more frugally and leaving the money in the bank. Overdrafts should be used to:

- provide working capital for the everyday trading you do;
- give you a little flexibility to cope with the unexpected.

Plenty of people start a business without an overdraft. Here are some examples.

- Engineer Malcolm used contract labour rather than employing a full-time team. He only had to pay people when he had work for them to do.
- Insurance broker Simon worked as a postman every morning, starting work in his own business at 10 a.m.
- Farm trader Raymond drove a lorry, doing business via his mobile phone during rest breaks along the way.

**CHAPTER 7**

# Be profitable

Ways to manage your margins

# 10 steps to improve your trading margins

Your trading margin is quite simply the difference between your selling price and the cost of providing the service or product. Your profit is the total margins less overhead costs. It's harder than you think to calculate your trading margins accurately. Here are ten steps to success.

1   **Timesheets** – always keep timesheets. It may seem like a chore but make it a habit. You need to know how much time you spend on a job. It's often longer than you realise!

2   **Materials** – record all materials you use job by job. Don't overlook the small things as these add up over time.

3   **Travel** – most customers are happy to pay your travel costs. Use HM Revenue & Customs (HMRC) rates or charge on your public transport costs.

4   **Mark-up** – you won't make a margin unless you build it in. Most people add a percentage mark-up to things sold on to the customer.

5   **Hourly rate** – solicitors, car repair workshops and plumbers all charge time at an hourly rate that reflects their knowledge, expertise and the market rate in their area. You must do the same.

6   **Bad debts** – if you suffer from bad debts, build a figure into your pricing so that all customers are covering the occasional non-payer. Budget for bad debts.

7   **Good buying** – don't pay too much for stuff. Negotiate the best deal you can with regular suppliers. The less you pay the more you make.

8   **Purchase orders** – having a piece of paper that your bookkeeper can match with a supplier's invoice prevents accidental overpayments if supplier invoices are wrong.

9   **Add what's new** – constantly review your costs. If things go up in price then reflect this in the prices you charge.

10  **Benchmark** – find others in your business sector and share data. Find out where their costs are lower. Trade organisations often do this for their members.

 **brilliant** **tip**

Don't be a 'busy fool'. In other words, avoid working long hours on things that don't make you money. Be selective!

## Common costing pitfalls to avoid

In some businesses more than others, it's far too easy to overlook some of your costs. This reduces your trading margin and you find yourself very busy but making little financial headway. Here are some examples to prompt you to avoid these pitfalls in your business.

● A management consultant travels widely and finds himself not charging for days spent on the road between clients.

● A training provider uses profiling software that is licensed but forgets to spread the licence fee over the 50 profiles they create.

● A service engineer uses very expensive, specialist lubricants but doesn't factor the cost into their price.

● A domiciliary care provider charges the same per hour for all jobs rather than charging a premium hourly rate for short visits. Short visits mean fewer hours worked in a day.

**brilliant** recap

Your selling will inevitably be a compromise between:

● your costs plus a healthy margin;
● market price for what you do; and
● the extent to which your reputation enables you to command a premium price.

# 10 things that erode your profits and how to avoid them

When you are growing a business, it's a battle to keep costs under control as your sales grow. The euphoria of sales success can lull you into a false sense of security. You focus on doing the work and not on your profitability. Here are ten things to watch out for.

1   **Overpromising** – we all do it. A customer places a huge order and wants delivery really quickly. To keep them happy you agree – then lose money attempting the impossible.

2   **Underdelivering** – you're busy and you cut corners. Work quality falls, mistakes are made and soon customers, and your reputation, begin to slip away.

3   **Paperwork getting left** – in the rush to get all the work done, you put off things like raising invoices. You forget to include all the costs and you find you're no longer making money.

4   **Last-minute buying** – you become so busy working that you don't plan your purchases. Lots of last-minute purchases at retail price are needed for the job, but hit your margin.

5   **Late payers** – the customer of your dreams becomes a haunting nightmare. Let down and disappointed, they stall on payment while arguing on quality.

6   **Learning curve** – you hire more staff to meet the demand but they take ages to train and output falls as your existing people help them learn. Your costs rise but not your output.

7   **Space race** – with all the extra staff, stock and equipment, suddenly there's no room. Temperatures rise, the car park is full and everybody starts to moan.

8   **Systems squeaking** – perhaps you've used a manual job card system or rudimentary accounts software. All this extra work means you need to upgrade. That takes time!

9   **Time travelling** – the hands on the clock spin round and you seem to be on an accelerating treadmill. As you get busier, things can actually take you longer. You're very tired.

10  **Partner's panicking** – all of a sudden, just when everything that can go wrong seems to, you get home and are met with a barrage of anxious questions from the love of your life.

Growing a business is not all bad news. You simply have to be alert to the fact that unless you've invested in people, plant and processes before winning those extra sales, then it's going to be tough for a while. Few successful entrepreneurs built their businesses that way. Most accepted the orders first and then invested in the capacity to meet them.

 **recap**

Your second customer will double your turnover. As you grow, it becomes easier because each new customer is joining a lengthening list.

Here are some of the positive things you can do to maintain profitability as you grow.

- **Schedule** – scheduling your work using specialist software, a spreadsheet or even a calendar on the wall enables you to allocate time and resources and to plan when things are needed. Tell customers when their job is scheduled so they know when you expect to deliver. Try building a forward order book – you may not need to do everything at once.

- **Communicate** – think about how leading e-commerce sites like Amazon email to confirm your order and expected delivery, and then again when the order is dispatched. If there's a problem you are informed straight away. You cannot be angry because you are kept informed – the firm is being honest and realistic. How could you communicate better?

- **Evaluate** – take time to look back on each job you do. Did you complete it within the budgeted material cost and time? (Did you measure the time it took?) Only by looking at what has happened can you change what will happen in the future. Create a culture of continuous improvement.

 **example**

**Jass Patel, Mokoko, St Albans, www.mokoko.biz**

Jass set up the cocktail bar Mokoko with the intention of being the best in the business. He skimped on nothing, especially the spirits his team mixed to make the drinks. Making a living but not a fortune, he successfully applied to appear on Channel Five's *The Business Inspector*.

Entrepreneur and presenter Hilary Devey took him to task for spending too much. She argued that his customers would not notice if he used cheaper spirits but his bottom line would. Together they ran some blind tastings and Hilary was proved right.

Jass realised that he was more discerning than his customers, reduced his own quality standards and saw his profitablity grow. He could have saved more if he'd bought basic own-label brands, but this was further than he was prepared to go.

# 10 things about trading terms it's good to bear in mind

The small print on the back of your estimates or invoices is just one aspect of trading terms. More important is that you set up deals in a way that makes it easy for your customer to pay you promptly and efficiently. Here are ten things you might try in order to ensure successful trading.

1   **Deposits** – if you're buying materials to fulfil an order it's not unreasonable to ask for some money up front. There's nothing wrong with asking for 30 per cent or more with the order.

2   **Pay on delivery** – why not ask for the balance on delivery? Many web designers, for example, will not post your new site on the internet until you've paid.

3   **Odd numbers** – if you ask for payment in 30 days you'll often wait until the end of the following month. Invoice for payment in 7, 14, 21 or 28 days and you'll get paid faster.

4   **Retainers** – if you do work for someone every month, why not ask them to set up a regular monthly payment? Work flow may vary but equal, regular payments help cash flow.

5   **Maintenance agreements** – charging an annual fee for maintenance means that you can service your customers' equipment when it suits you. This reduces inconvenient emergency call-outs and helps keep your customers loyal. Everyone wins.

6   **Annual increases** – tell customers that you review (increase) your prices annually. This prevents you from having to raise the subject because an annual increase is expected.

7   **Incentives** – if referrals are how you win new clients, offer an incentive to reward those who make introductions. Happy customers are usually happy to recommend you if asked.

8   **Prompt payment discount** – add a standard 5 per cent surcharge to your invoice and then show this as a discount for payment-within terms. Most will then pay promptly.

9   **Statements** – seen by many as a cop-out from chasing debts, there is no doubt that many companies pay only when they get a statement, so send one in good time.

10  **Use the phone** – whatever your terms of business there really is no better way of making sure you get paid on time. Polite, pressing phoning prompts payment.

You will notice that the focus of the preceding checklist is on getting payment. Cash is the lifeblood of any business and when you are growing you simply cannot have too much of it.

 **tip**

No amount of small print in your trading terms will substitute for following the tips on the previous page. Actions are always more effective than words.

## How to ask for payment

It's never easy to ask for the money. Here are a few lines you might find useful.

- Your job was one of our biggest this month and your payment is important to our cash flow. Tell me, when can I expect to see the cheque?
- We had to call in a few favours from suppliers to meet your deadline and don't want to keep them waiting for their money. First, though, I need to ask you to pay us. Tell me, when can I expect to see the cheque?
- We're about to invest in a new XYZ, which will enable us to do an even better job for you. However, I need to show our bank that we're good at getting the money in. So please, could you send me that cheque?
- Look, I'm working alongside your guys and they got paid last month but I didn't. It's really embarrassing for me. Why have you not paid me yet?

Others will tell you all sorts of gimmicky ways of chasing overdue payments. Avoid trying to be clever – be honest and open instead.

## Credit cards

Do not underestimate the value of accepting credit card payments. Many young businesses use them as a line of credit, so why not take payments in this way yourself? Although you will pay a commission to your provider (merchant), you will get the money up front, while your customer may have up to 60 days to pay. Credit cards are also very convenient and you know straight away if the card company refuses the transaction.

Remember that you need one merchant account for sales where the customer is present and another for online trading.

 **tip**

PayPal is universally used by small businesses to process online payments. There are also other similar providers. There is no excuse for not accepting card payments.

# 10 quick ways to increase your profitability

With so many of the things we buy it is the extras that make the profit for the provider. What's more, it is often the optional extras that differentiate the product in the marketplace. Cars and first-class travel are good examples. Here are ten extras you might use to increase profitability.

1   **Morning delivery** – people will pay extra for quicker delivery. All you do is rearrange your driver's route to go there first. Your costs stay the same but the profits rise.

2   **Changes** – every time a customer has a change of mind it creates work. Even if it doesn't, make it obvious that it's a change and charge for it. People will pay for changes.

3   **Overtime** – if you have to incur higher labour costs to meet customers' deadlines, should they not pay more? You can often charge more for a 'rushed job'.

4   **Assembly** – so many people just do what they always do and forget to look for opportunities. If you make components, why not see if you can handle assembly as well?

5   **Disbursements** – solicitors have a wonderful way of recording every phone call and postage stamp – and then calling them 'disbursements' and charging. Do the same.

6   **Packaging** – environmental legislation makes packaging disposal a real headache for many. If you make regular deliveries, collect used packaging and recycle or reuse.

7   **Just ask** – Indian restaurants seem to offer you extras instinctively – poppadoms, pickles, side dishes, more beer. They understand that the more they offer, the more you will buy.

8   **Assume** – add things to the order and give the customer the chance to opt out. Most will buy. A good example is the travel insurance added by online rail ticket sellers.

9   **Time** – this is your biggest cost. If a job is completed in less time than you estimated, do not automatically pass the saving on to the customer. Benefit from your efficiency.

10   **Offer choices** – even if two options cost you the same, you can always ask more for the most popular. Price should be linked to demand, not cost.

The golden rule when pricing your work is always to base your price on market conditions. Too many people simply tally up their costs and add a margin. You will find that if you set your prices to reflect market conditions, some things you make or sell will earn you more than others. That's fine and, at times, you can use part of this extra margin to encourage people to try new products. This is achieved by offering 'buy one get one free' or similar deals.

You therefore need a range of products or services to be able to give your customers choice. By giving choices, you make it harder for them to say no. Your product or service ranges should contain:

- a low cost, entry-level option – allowing new customers a low risk trial;
- a high cost, top flight option – making everything else look better value;
- a mid-range cost option with various choices – where most of your work is done;
- optional extras – profit-laden add-ons.

More examples of adding extras are shown in the table below.

| Product or service | High-margin added extra |
| --- | --- |
| Bicycle hire | Maps |
| Premixed concrete | Shuttering |
| Hotel | Flowers and chocolates in room |
| Car maintenance | Valeting |

Remember that you can always discount extras from time to time to create incentives.

**CHAPTER 8**

# Manage cash flow

Keeping the business going

# 10 simple tips for a healthy cash flow

Many people will say that cash is the lifeblood of a business. This is because without cash flowing into the business, none can flow out. Here's how to make sure you keep your cash flow healthy.

1   **Invoice promptly** – as soon as you've finished a job, send in the bill. Don't wait until the end of the month to raise your invoices.

2   **Get paid on time** – your invoice can get 'lost in the system' of a big organisation and overlooked in a busy small one. A polite phone call when the money is due increases your chance of getting paid on time.

3   **Pay slowly** – it makes sense not to be too quick to pay your bills. Over time you get to know who you can delay and who to pay on time.

4   **Avoid direct debits** – many of your regular suppliers, particularly energy suppliers, like to be paid by direct debit. Pay when it suits you, not others!

5   **Sell more** – obvious really, but the higher your sales the more likely you are to have money in the bank.

6   **Spend less** – the flip side of selling more is that your costs go up. Make sure you renegotiate what you pay for stuff if you find yourself buying more. It all helps.

7   **Keep work flowing** – work in progress can kill your cash flow. You've sold lots, you're working hard and just can't get things out of the door as fast as you once could. You're now buying more quickly and invoicing more slowly!

8   **Avoid bad debts** – some people are easy to sell to as they don't have the money themselves to pay. Maybe they're on 'stop' with their usual supplier so come to you.

9   **Buy 'just in time'** – and don't carry more stock than you need. Try to order things as you need them.

10  **Have a sale!** – declutter your business by selling off old stock, damaged goods and anything else you no longer need.

## Credit checking

Many business advisers will encourage you to credit check new customers. It's also good practice to set a credit limit for each customer. This means you can limit your exposure to bad debt. It can also mean you remember to ask for the money before accepting the next order.

It's easier to credit check incorporated companies than sole traders or partnerships. That's because they have to file annual accounts. These are available online via a number of subscription service credit referencing agencies. You simply sign up to be able to search online.

The problem with credit checking is that it is based on historical data. This means a company can look OK but actually be far from able to pay its debts.

Simple ways to check if your customers are likely to become a bad credit risk include:

- reading your local business newspaper as these often list court judgments;
- asking for credit references from existing suppliers;
- suggesting they pay via credit card as this gives you the money now and gives your customer the option of paying the card company later.

**brilliant** recap

A deal's just a promise until the customer's money is in your bank.

# 10 situations where you need to focus harder on cash flow

We all get into a business routine and cash flow can be smooth and uneventful for years. However, there are a number of situations you can find yourself in where things can change quickly. Here are ten situations to look out for.

1   **When you start** – you'll always have more costs than you planned for. Watch your cash flow in the early months until you and your business get into a routine.

2   **When you grow** – growing businesses often run out of money. Quite simply, your outgoings grow before the extra sales you've won translate into money in the bank.

3   **At Christmas** – December is a short month during which most firms close down for almost two weeks. Everyone's chasing money in December and there's usually less to invoice too.

4   **In January** – Christmas credit card bills and tax to pay for the self-employed make January a tight month for many. January is always a difficult month in which to get money in.

5   **In recession** – when the economy dips, it's like throwing a rock into a pond. Those in the middle get hit hardest, but even on the edge the ripples can cause you problems.

6   **When competition hots up** – if a new rival appears on the scene you may need to react to this competitive threat. Make sure you don't get pushed out of profitability.

7   **If you get ill** – for the one-person business, sickness, bereavement and a wealth of other personal problems can slow your income but not your costs.

8   **When it snows** – bad weather of all kinds can hit your cash flow. Snow keeps people at home and nobody buys an umbrella when the sun is shining. Plan for the seasons.

9   **When legislation looms** – at times, new rules come along that bump up your costs.

10  **When VAT is due** – if you're registered for VAT you have to pay over the tax you've collected over the past three months. VAT can get 'lost' in your cash flow – plan for VAT payments.

## Arranging bank loans

Too many people use overdraft finance to cover long-term debt. That's because it's often easier to increase the overdraft than to arrange a loan. Here are a few things you need to have in place before applying for a loan.

- Your business plan should be up to date.
- Cash flow projections that show the future with and without the loan.
- Both an optimistic and a pessimistic forecast.
- A 'plan B' if the investment doesn't work for both you and the lender.

## brilliant    tip

If you jointly own your home and your partner refuses to offer it as security for a bank loan, you may well qualify for support under the Enterprise Finance Guarantee Scheme. The reason is that the asset is jointly owned and both owners need to consent to its being used as security. Encouraging your partner to refuse to allow you to borrow against the family home can make it less problematical if your business partner has no assets against which to secure business borrowing. Exposure to different degrees of financial risk can damage the relationships between business partners when things get tough.

# 10 ways to deal with running out of cash

Fast-growing businesses sometimes run out of cash. It's one of the major reasons why businesses fail. Quite simply, as turnover grows so does demand for working capital – you're really busy, selling lots, but run out of money. Here are ten ways to avoid it.

1   **See it coming** – if you use a spreadsheet to forecast your cash flow accurately, you will see the danger signs a few months in advance. Act early and avoid the worst.

2   **Chase your debts** – when you are really busy, chasing customers for payment often slips down the priority list. Always find time to get the cash in.

3   **Stall suppliers** – everyone starts paying late when things get tight. However, clever people negotiate deferred payment with their supplier first, rather than simply stall.

4   **Focus on the profitable** – if you have unprofitable activities or products, consider ditching them. Too often we hang on to the stuff (and customers!) we should really let go.

5   **Tell the bank** – make sure you have a plan and can show that you're on top of the situation. Banks will often provide short-term additional finance.

6   **Shift stock** – look around and see if you're carrying stock you could quickly liquidate. Sell the stuff you no longer need. Take junk to an auction and get rid of it.

7   **Take a salary holiday** – stopping your own pay for a month or so shows those around you that you are committed to winning. When things are fixed, take a bonus!

8   **Defer VAT** – talk to those you pay taxes to and explain the situation. They'll often negotiate a deferred payment deal to help you out. Always ask first. They get angry if you don't!

9   **Avoid using prepayments** – watch out that you're not using prepayments for future work to pay for supplies used to meet today's orders. This might indicate that you're insolvent.

10  **Get tough** – you need to squeeze money back into your cash flow. Maybe there are things you could actually do without? Batten down the hatches and chuck excess expense overboard.

## What bank managers say about cash flow problems

Bankers see people hit the wall all the time. They say that when cash gets tight, it's because the business owner:

- has no proper cash flow forecast so is caught out when it's almost too late;
- takes it personally and goes into denial, ignoring the risk and getting angry;
- blames others and fails to recognise the need to change the way they operate;
- panics and becomes less efficient, risking customer and supplier goodwill;
- gives up the fight before they've even started.

The art is to see danger coming and trim your business to weather the storm. You need to prepare a cash flow forecast that allows you to see the impact on your overdraft of sharp increases in sales, delays in customer payments and rises in your business costs. Many business-support organisations and banks can give you prepared spreadsheets into which you simply enter your own figures. These are great – they also form a checklist for the things you might otherwise overlook. People often forget to include in their cash flow forecasting:

- VAT payments, due quarterly;
- VAT collected on sales;
- employer's National Insurance;
- quarterly payments – for example, machinery leases;
- repayments of existing loans.

# 10 ways to ask for overdue payment

Many people find it uncomfortable to ask for money. Remember that if the customer has had the goods or service, the money you're asking them for is actually yours. Don't feel bad – instead use one or more of these proven methods to get paid.

1  **Ask** – obvious though it sounds, many people are reluctant to ask for money, choosing instead to write or send statements. Avoid using euphemisms – ask for the money!

2  **Statements** – some companies only pay when a statement arrives. Send them statements early.

3  **Know who** – establish rapport with the person who actually handles each significant customer's payments. Get to know them and make sure they put you at the top of the pile.

4  **Pop in** – if you sell to the public it's always best to get paid when you've finished the job. If you find yourself waiting for payment, call round and collect the cheque.

5  **Ring at home** – Companies House can tell you where directors live. If you've been unable to get through to them at work, look up their home phone number and ring them in the evening. Of course it's obtrusive, but that's why it works!

6  **Solicitors** – many law firms offer a debt-chasing service. These can be effective.

7  **Avoid emotion** – however angry or let down you feel, don't lose your temper. It doesn't help matters; in fact it can make them worse.

8  **Small claim** – it is a simple, but lengthy, process to take a customer to the Small Claims Court. You can do it yourself but be prepared to argue your case in front of a judge.

9  **Garnishee order** – if the customer is going bust, getting a garnishee order from the court means you get paid directly when their customers pay them.

10 **Move on** – it's the small debts that always annoy the most. Every month they take time, cause anxiety and simply sit on your books. Write off small bad debts and move on.

Managing customer expectations is the key to getting paid. A gentle reminder phone call ahead of the due date can make sure your invoice filters through to the accounts team in time.

If you sell one-off products or services then you need to spell out to the customer what your trading terms are. This is best done when the order is placed and confirmed.

When asking for payment:

● have the figures to hand and make sure they're accurate;

● remain polite and objective;

● if there's a problem with your product or service, apologise and fix it, then ask again;

● listen sympathetically to the reasons for late payment you hear;

● be realistic and compassionate if the reason for delay is genuine.

## Taking someone to court

If all else fails and you're still owed money, it might be worth taking your customer to court. In some cases you can do this very conveniently online (see **www.hmcourts-service.gov.uk**).

Only start court proceedings if you are confident that:

● your invoice was fair and has not and cannot be disputed;

● you have tried asking for the money and the promised payment has not arrived;

● your customer has the money (a court order will not prompt payment if the money is simply not there to pay).

 **tip**

Although it is relatively easy to start legal proceedings to have a creditor made bankrupt, it is rarely worth the effort. Do not let your anger cloud your objectivity.

## CHAPTER 9

# Control costs

How to earn more by
spending less

# 10 reasons why it's smart to manage your costs

Everyone focuses on winning sales and growing turnover, but often the biggest opportunity to boost profit is by reducing your costs. As Jass Patel found in the Mokoko cocktail bar example in Chapter 7, you can reduce costs without reducing perceived quality. Here are ten reasons why you might choose to do the same.

1  **Profit** – quite simply, the lower your costs, the higher your profits.

2  **Scale** – the more profitable your business, the easier it will be to manage. You're making more money from less activity.

3  **Risk** – the more you sell, the more you're exposed to bad debt. Better to make your profit on lower sales.

4  **Quality** – remember that buying better doesn't always mean spending less. You want reliability, durability and consistency if you're to avoid customer complaints.

5  **Buying is important** – it sounds silly, but we all overlook how important buying is. If your sales are £100,000 and your profit and pay total £40,000, you're actually spending £60,000. More than any one customer spends with you!

6  **Staff count** – in most businesses, staff form the largest cost. Employing people is expensive. See Chapters 15 and 16 for top people tips.

7  **You borrow less** – if you spend less, you need less working capital. Remember that money costs you too – it's called interest!

8  **Every little counts** – it's easy to let your costs run away with you, especially the small things like subscriptions and gadgets. Little costs together make big costs!

9  **Space** – if you carry a lot of stock you need more space. It sounds obvious but buying stuff as you need it might mean you can do away with storage space altogether.

10 **Save energy** – for most of us, energy and fuel costs are an increasing burden. Don't overlook them.

 **brilliant** tip

There's a lot of truth in the old adage, 'Turnover is vanity; profit is sanity'.

## Adding value through what you buy

It is important to manage costs. But sometimes, what you buy is more important than what you pay for it. People will often pay a premium for products and services that contain branded components that are themselves considered premium brands. Examples include:

● **Intel** – people will pay more for a PC with an Intel chip because they believe (from Intel's own marketing) that the chip will perform better than cheaper rivals;

● **Smart** – a Smart car might cost more to buy than other, similar sized models, but people on holiday will pay a premium to hire a car they think will be more fun;

● **MBA** – a consultancy will pay staff with MBAs higher salaries; they will also be able to charge them out at higher day rates.

 **example**

**Funchal Car Hire, Madeira, www.funchalcarhire.net**

Madeira is popular with middle-aged, well-off northern European tourists. The weather is good all year round and you're unlikely to get mugged or an upset tummy.

If you'd visited in August 2010 and decided to hire a car for one week, this is what it would have cost you:

Fiat Panda – £168

Smart Pulse – £223

Few car hire companies have Smart cars on Madeira and tourists like them. Funchal Car Hire can charge a premium price and know that the cars will always be booked. The Fiat Panda, on the other hand, is simply 'another small car' and its low rental cost reflects the fact that this is a commodity product, often hired on arrival in the airport arrivals lounge.

What is interesting is that the easier to rent car, that costs more, actually pays for itself sooner than the cheaper Fiat (see below).

|  | Rental | Cost new | No. of weeks' hire to cover purchase price |
|---|---|---|---|
| Fiat Panda | £168 | £7,600 | 45 |
| Smart Pulse | £223 | £8,800 | 39 |

You can see straight away that the Smart car is more profitable for the car hire company.

# 10 tips to help you work better with your suppliers

Your suppliers are as important to you as your customers. This is true if you are a manufacturer buying components or a consultancy with freelance associates. You'll work best with suppliers that have these ten qualities.

1   **Reliability** – your reputation hangs on your suppliers' ability to meet your needs. If they let you down, you end up letting your customers down. Make sure they're reliable.

2   **Tolerance** – you are unlikely to be perfect either! Good suppliers tolerate those panic phone calls and try their best to get you out of a muddle – even when it's self-inflicted.

3   **Potential** – you want suppliers who can grow with you. They should share your ambition and be prepared to invest in keeping up with you. Notice if you outgrow a supplier.

4   **Quality** – buy the best your customers need. Don't encourage suppliers to cut corners to reduce costs. Nor buy better than you need. Check quality regularly.

5   **Stability** – you want your supplier to be there when you need them. Take an interest in their aspirations, achievements and challenges. Help them grow if you can.

6   **Good suppliers** – your supplier buys as well as sells. How good are their suppliers?

7   **Deep pockets** – when your cash flow hiccups, the first people you lean on for credit are your suppliers. Can they support you in times of trouble?

8   **Great people** – any business is only as good as its people. Good suppliers have motivated, able, enthusiastic people. Get to know the people who work on your behalf.

9   **Enquiring minds** – nothing stays the same for long. You want suppliers that are constantly seeking improvement. Are yours exploring new and innovative ideas?

10  **Fun** – you will get more from your suppliers if their people socialise with your people. Why not challenge them to five-a-side football?

Finding good suppliers is as important as finding good customers. In fact, to enjoy success you need both. Some places you might look are:

● trade journals;

● industry exhibitions;

● local business networks;

- the internet;
- competitors' products (to identify component suppliers);
- professional and trade organisations (to identify associates);
- friends in similar businesses to yourself – ask for recommendations;
- foreign trade missions able to introduce overseas suppliers;
- university research teams working in your industry area;
- newspapers reporting business achievement.

## Be a good customer

You'll get the best deal and support if you are considered a good customer by your suppliers. Here's how.

- Agree annual targets and work together to achieve them.
- Confirm orders in writing and make them clear and specific.
- Don't blame your suppliers for your own mistakes.
- Pay when you say you will. If payment is delayed for any reason, let your supplier know as soon as you can.
- Give constructive feedback to encourage innovation.

### brilliant example

**Barnwell Printers, www.barnwellprint.co.uk**

Julian and his brother Lincoln Barnwell are printers. Their firm was established by their great-grandfather and they are very much part of their local business scene. Not content to rest on the laurels of previous generations, they have invested substantially in premises, plant and people.

Julian is never complacent about his role as a supplier. His quotations are delivered quickly, the customer always knows where their job is in the production process and he watches his rivals all the time.

Keen on water sports, Julian invested in equipment for his speedboat that enables even novice water-skiers to succeed. Most summer weekends he is out with customers teaching them a new skill and building the bond of trust between them.

# 10 tips for managing what you spend on customers

It may seem obvious, but managing what you spend on your customers will dictate both how profitable the transaction is and how happy your customers are. It's a new way to view your business costs. Here are ten things to look out for.

1   **Trust** – the best thing customers can give you is their trust. In return, you must be honest and trust them too. Win their trust and they'll only ask you to provide what you both agree is fair.

2   **Tolerance** – a little give and take on both sides will enable you to avoid last-minute panic buying. Encourage your customers to work with you and be more tolerant if things go wrong.

3   **Potential** – a customer business that is growing can give you much more. You might invest more in pleasing customers with growth potential.

4   **Status** – some people want the best 'branded' offer and others are happy with cheaper 'own brand' solutions. Match your offer to customer expectations – one size won't fit all.

5   **Referrals** – why not offer incentives to your customers to introduce new ones? For example, a website offers a free month's subscription to subscribers signing up a new member.

6   **Good address** – be wary of making assumptions about customer expectations based on where they live or run their business. Better to match their budget!

7   **Vision** – help your customers develop their vision for the future. Make sure you feature in it. It always costs less to service an existing customer than to develop a new one.

8   **Faults** – if you fix things for your customers that were not strictly your problem, they'll be more lenient when things go wrong with what you deliver. Fixing problems costs money!

9   **Fun** – Plato said you could learn more from an hour's play than a year's conversation. Have fun with your customers; find out where they think you could save costs. Pass some, but not all, savings on.

10  **Good payers** – you'll make more margin from a customer who pays you on time. The interest costs you pick up when they pay late are a business cost you'll want to reduce.

## Easy ways to reduce the cost of servicing your customers

Of course, in an ideal world your customers will find you. This is more certainly the case if you have a retail business that relies on passing trade. However much your customer group is self-selecting, it's good to encourage the people you want to do business with and discourage those who make you less profit. This chapter is about managing your costs and so we need to focus on how you can make more profit from each customer. Here are some ways to encourage existing customers to make you more profit by costing you less.

- **Take fewer, larger consignments** – it's usually cheaper to make up bigger orders.

- **Simplify your range** – the more different things you make or do, the more stock you need and the more complex your organisation. Cut out marginal activities.

- **Let go of the small customers you've outgrown** – and spend the time you save winning new, bigger ones.

 **tip**

Your customers are looking at the value you give, not the costs you have incurred. Make sure they understand why some things cost more than they expect.

# 10 types of tax you need to know about

Nobody likes paying taxes, but they are a cost to your business all the same. It often pays to take professional advice to minimise your tax liability. Remember though that your business should focus on maximising your profit opportunity, not reducing your tax burden. Note too that there is a fine line to tread between the good practice of 'tax avoidance' and the illegal practice of 'tax evasion'. Here are ten tax basics you need to know.

1  **Income tax** – you have probably paid this at some point as an employee. It is deducted from your pay and sent to HM Revenue & Customs (HMRC) on your behalf. As an employer you do the deducting and sending. It's rarely worth calculating yourself – use a bureau service instead. If you run a limited company you will pay income tax too.

2  **Self-assessment** – this is what you do as a self-employed person or partner in an unincorporated firm. You then pay your 'income' tax in two lumps, in January and July. Your accountant can help you to complete the forms, or you can do it yourself online.

3  **National Insurance** – this tax affects both employees and employers. Employers pay this to HMRC. Never be tempted to make them wait for tax payments – tax officials can get very angry very quickly!

4  **VAT** – if your sales exceed a certain threshold you have to register for and charge VAT. This can be a real problem if you sell to customers who cannot reclaim the tax as a business might. However, once registered you can reclaim VAT that others charge you.

5  **Business rates** – this tax is charged on business premises and collected by the local authority. Some landlords include it in the rent.

6  **Corporation tax** – limited companies and PLCs pay this. It is levied on profits and can be reduced by investing in equipment that can be depreciated against the tax liability.

7  **Cars and vans** – if you are a director or employee of your business and the business runs your car, you will be taxed on it as a 'benefit in kind'. If you are self-employed the deal is usually better. If you use your own car in your business you can pay yourself certain tax-free allowances towards the running costs.

8  **Expenses** – if you incur expenses, say for rail travel in connection with your business, you can pay yourself back. You need to keep receipts and not claim personal expenses.

9   **Overseas taxes** – when you buy or sell outside the UK, particularly outside Europe, you may incur additional tax liabilities. Your local Chamber of Commerce can advise you.

10  **Cash** – tax officials know what kinds of business have the most cash transactions. They can calculate what your sales should be from your purchases. Don't pocket the cash!

## Accountants

The cost of a good accountant is almost always recouped by the amount of tax saved. Many allow you to pay them in monthly instalments so you hardly notice the annual bill when it arrives. Choosing the right accountant for you and your business is really important. Here are some pointers to help you find the best for you.

● **Recommendation** – ask people you like and respect who they use and why.

● **Local** – it's usually best to choose someone nearby because it's easier to visit each other.

● **Appropriate** – choose an accountant who works with businesses of the size you plan to be. This makes it less likely that you'll outgrow your accountant.

● **Values** – we all have different values, attitudes and opinions. Choosing an accountant who thinks the way that you do will help you both get on.

● **Price** – don't choose on price because cheapest isn't always best.

**CHAPTER 10**

# Go to work

How to find premises, or work
successfully at home

# 10 good reasons not to pay for an office

Working from home is incredibly convenient. It also saves you the cost and hassle of finding somewhere to base your business. Of course, you need some space and there may be distractions, but there are many good reasons for working from home. Here are ten of them.

1   **Cheap** – the money you save by not renting an office can be invested instead in technology, marketing and other things that build your business.

2   **Commuting** – travelling a few feet to the office each day can feel great after years of catching the 07.30 train. You can work longer hours in shorter days.

3   **Convenient** – if you are the creative type, or just prefer to work at odd times, working from home means you can go into the office or workshop whenever you want.

4   **Childcare** – while something of a two-edged sword, working from home makes childcare a lot easier. Why not create workspace for your kids too? Make it fun!

5   **Coffee shops** – for many of us these days, coffee shops provide a convenient place to meet clients, or simply catch up with our emails. Find yourself a favourite coffee shop, get to know the staff and make it your home from home.

6   **Crises** – life is littered with domestic crises. It can be useful to be at home working during the day, even if it's only to let the plumber in when he calls to mend a tap.

7   **Comfortable** – OK, you need to create a work-like environment, but when you're having a day at the office you can dress down as far as you like.

8   **Colleagues** – you will undoubtedly have people who work with you either regularly or on a project basis. Use Skype for video conferencing and to keep in touch. Create a virtual office network.

9   **Environment** – if you like to listen to music you can. You can also have the windows open in winter or the heating on in summer. You can create the work environment you want.

10  **Colds** – you know when someone starts sneezing in an open-plan office? Soon everyone's reaching for the tissues. Working from home can be healthy too!

 **tip**

Don't just use the chain coffee shops to meet people. That's what everybody does. Consider cafés at art galleries and tourist attractions too. Find a place that matches your business style.

## Self-discipline and loneliness

Some people find working alone a challenge. They get lonely and find themselves easily distracted. If you suffer from 'cabin fever', here are some ways to avoid it.

- **Share** – rent a desk in someone else's office. They don't have to be working in the same business, just someone, like you, who wants a work buddy.
- **Hot-desk** – most business centres provide hot-desking. This enables you to pay for space only when you're using it. You'll also find meeting rooms, telephone answering and a postal address if you need it.
- **Empty office** – sometimes your best customer will happily give you workspace in exchange for the convenience of having you on site. You can 'earn' your rent.
- **Clubs** – major cities all have business clubs you can join. These cost more than basic hot-desking but provide a more personal service. Other members might also become clients.

 **tip**

If you work from home make sure you:

- have office contents and public liability insurance;
- remember that you can offset some household bills against your profits;
- have a separate work phone number and answer it professionally.

## brilliant example

**Alison Withers, www.alisonwithers.co.uk**

When Alison was made redundant after a long and successful career as a journalist, she knew she wanted to work from home. She now works freelance doing copywriting, editing and managing web content for a range of different clients. Working from home gives Alison flexibility, low overheads and, perhaps most importantly, peace and quiet when she needs to concentrate.

# 10 ways to look bigger than a one-man band

When you're pitching for really big contracts, it can pay to encourage people to think your business is actually bigger than it is. Customers want to know you're professional and have the back-up you need to deliver what you promise. Here are ten ways to look bigger than you are.

1   **Good address** – if you work from home, adapt your address to make it look like a business address. Prospect House, Station Road sounds much better than 123b Station Road.

2   **Phone answering** – have your phone diverted to a call-answering service when you are out. This is more reliable and more professional than forwarding calls to your mobile.

3   **Share facilities** – if you rent part of a building and another tenant has a better meeting room than you, borrow it when important clients visit.

4   **Website** – your virtual business environment should always be a few steps ahead of reality. Websites are cheaper than premises and are usually visited more often.

5   **Nice car** – however hard we try not to, we all judge our visitors by the cars they drive. If you usually go to visit your customers, make sure you drive a nice car. Also keep it clean!

6   **Think big** – your words will give you away. Make sure you think, talk and walk big. Always talk your business up, but never say anything that is not completely true.

7   **Associates** – a network of associates gives you manpower when you need it, and no overhead costs when you don't. Create a network of freelancers able to help.

8   **Branding** – if subcontractors visit your customers, perhaps as service engineers or to make deliveries, have your livery on their vehicles. Make it a condition of contract.

9   **Be proactive** – take control of your customer communication. If you call them before they need to ring you, they won't know that you're not always there to answer the phone.

10  **Bluff** – in reality, big firms can be less efficient than small ones. The art is to say 'Yes, no problem' to the customer and then sort out how to make it happen later. We all 'wing it'!

## Does size really matter?

It's easy to think that your customers will prefer a larger firm. This is rarely the case. All they really want is to get the job done, in time, on budget and without any problems. The vast majority of businesses in the UK (and across the world) are small. If you need reassuring that small is beautiful, remember that it's good to have the following.

- **Low overheads** – small businesses have small overheads and can often charge less.

- **Customers who feel valued** – with a small company each customer is important.

- **Flexibility** – if you're small you can quickly adapt to new opportunities.

- **Control** – you're the boss and can make decisions. That makes you more responsive to your customers' changing needs.

- **Transparency** – with a small business, what the customer sees is what they get.

### brilliant example

**Michelle Greenwood, www.nonamefoodcompany.co.uk**

Wanting to combine a love of cooking with raising two children, Michelle started a catering business based in her kitchen at home. The business grew, and so did the children. When they started school she moved her business to a local golf club. Here she had more space and a captive market for her food. Both the club and her business benefited.

Her reputation quickly grew and now Michelle's business is well established and widely respected. Moving the business from home to a place where she'd meet lots of potential customers is one of the reasons she's become so successful.

# 10 things to look out for before renting or leasing

As your business grows you will almost inevitably need premises. Unless you are able to buy a place you will need to rent or lease somewhere. Here are ten things to look out for.

1  **Long lease** – you probably don't want a long lease. Too long and you might find it difficult to move if you outgrow the place. Too short and you might be asked to move on before you're ready.

2  **Break clauses** – make sure your lease contains break clauses. These are opportunities to 'break' the lease and move out. Many leases have an annual 'break clause'.

3  **Repairs** – check whether you are to be liable for repairs. Repairs can be expensive!

4  **Rates** – it's easy to forget that you'll also be paying local authority business rates. These can be high, particularly for retail premises.

5  **Service charge** – if you're in a shared complex you will probably be asked to pay a service charge to cover things like maintenance, cleaning and heating.

6  **Power** – many business centre landlords individually meter and mark up electricity, gas and telephone to their tenants. Check the detail before you sign.

7  **What's next door?** – don't just look at the place you're renting. Make sure there's nothing nearby that will cause you problems. A call centre next to a workshop might be a problem.

8  **Restrictions** – sometimes your lease or agreement will exclude some activities you might want to carry out. Check the small print carefully.

9  **Security** – make sure your insurer is happy with the security. You don't want to find yourself paying to upgrade what your landlord has installed.

10  **Parking** – your staff might all come to work by bus, but if they do come by car, is there enough parking for them? If your customers drive to you, where will they park?

Most landlords use a standard lease that is simply adapted for each unit. Leases are legal documents and there are often fees associated with setting one up. It is always wise to take independent legal advice before signing a lease for premises.

## A place of your own

Once your business is established and on track you might think about buying your own place. Buying your own business premises can make sense for the following reasons.

- You're buying an asset.

- Your rent payments become an investment not a cost.

- Rents go up over time. Your property loan will diminish.

- If you buy the property, your business can pay you rent.

- It's often possible to buy your business premises through a pension scheme. This can be very tax efficient.

**brilliant** tip

Don't confuse buying business premises with building your business. Only consider buying business premises if you know you can afford it without risking your enterprise's cash flow.

## Buy to let

Business premises can also make a good investment for your business. One successful entrepreneur who preferred not to be named in a case study has run a printing business for 20 years. Initially he rented a large unit on an edge-of-town business park.

When he could afford to, he bought the building from his landlord. Over the following years he also bought many of the other units on the business park. His neighbours became his tenants, and when premises became empty he found it easy to re-let them.

He found it very convenient to have his investment properties close to where he worked. He could easily keep an eye on things and was never far away if he needed to resolve a problem. Not surprisingly, most of his tenants also became customers of his printing business.

# 10 workspace ideas you might not have considered

Where you work is important. You're going to spend a lot of time there and you want to feel comfortable. Equally, it's important not to get carried away and spend money you don't have on things you can do without. Here are ten more workspace ideas you might not have considered.

1    **Loft** – if you want to work from home but have no space, why not convert the loft or cellar? You gain a space to work and add to the value of your home.

2    **Garden room** – you can buy portable garden offices that arrive ready to work in. This means you can keep work separate from family life and commute down the garden path.

3    **Garage** – clear the junk out of the garage and you have the perfect craft workshop, dog grooming parlour or studio. Clients can visit without having to feel they're visiting your home.

4    **Go mobile** – hairdressers, personal trainers, plumbers and many other tradespeople and professionals avoid the need for premises by visiting their customers. Many customers will pay a premium to have the convenience of a home visit.

5    **On the move** – think about those roadside cafes set up on a converted bus. Why not convert a van into a hairdressing salon, carpet shop or consulting room?

6    **Short let** – if location is less important than having lots of space, you can often get short-term leases on premises due for conversion.

7    **Supplier/customer's place** – want to open a cafe? Why not take over the staff canteen in a business centre or office block? You then have space and a captive marketplace.

8    **Village hall** – community owned buildings are often empty for much of the time. You could rent workspace or, if you work with groups, organise a programme at several halls.

9    **Family or friends** – you may not have space but what about your parents' spare room? Could you work from their home and combine business with duty visits?

10   **Virtual** – some people work entirely virtually. They rely on their laptop and mobile phone to stay in touch and work wherever they happen to be. Some customers like this and others dislike the suggested transience of working in this way.

## brilliant    recap

Your business needs a base only if the work you do demands it. What customers want most of all is to know how to find you. Where you are is probably less important than you think.

## brilliant    example

**Roadside haircuts**

If you drive along the A11 in South Norfolk you'll often see a blue barber's van in a layby. The owner provides no-nonsense haircuts to truckers. The drivers seem to know his schedule and time a rest-break rendezvous when in need of a trim. His van is very old but fully equipped. The owner knows that drivers often work long hours and don't want to waste precious home time getting their hair cut. He does it when they have to take a roadside break and would otherwise be reading the paper. A town centre shop would be more costly for him and less convenient for his customers.

**CHAPTER 11**

# Market yourself

## Understand why people buy

# 10 things your customers will look for

People don't buy things for what they are but for what they will do for them. They need to be convinced that the benefits will outweigh the cost. It doesn't matter what your product or service is, or if you sell to businesses or consumers. People buy benefits, not features. In other words, what it does is more important than what it is. Here are ten benefits that customers will be looking for.

1  **Meeting a need** – the greater the need, the easier the sale. For example, you'll be keener to find a glazier if you have a broken window.

2  **Convenience** – think about an ice cream van on a hot sun-drenched beach. You want something cold and will buy what's there, even if it costs more. You'll pay a premium for the convenience.

3  **Affordability** – however big the benefit, your customer needs to be able to afford to buy. If this is a problem, offer payment by instalments – or better, take credit card payment.

4  **Safety** – your product is reliable and perhaps reduces a risk that worries the customer.

5  **Performance** – it does what it says on the box. Reputation and evidence of performance, perhaps testimonials, will reassure your customers and help them say yes.

6  **Appearance** – it looks good. Given the choice, no one would buy an ugly product if one that looked more appealing was available. Also, does it make the customer look good?

7  **Comprehensible** – it is easy to use. You understand how to use it, but will your customer?

8  **Economical** – once you've bought it, how cheap will it be to run? A more concentrated product might cost more but be cheaper to use in the long run.

9  **Durable** – the lifespan of a product often dictates its value for money. The cheapest often does not last as long as the most expensive. You might need to spell this out.

10  **Trend** – nobody likes to feel left behind. This applies equally to business and consumer purchases. People like to follow fashion.

## Features and benefits

Understanding the difference between features and benefits is a key point. Too many people promote features and forget the benefits. Imagine you are buying a van. Here are some possible features and benefits.

| Feature | Benefit |
| --- | --- |
| Carries two tonnes | More deliveries possible per day |
| Diesel engine | Lower fuel cost per mile, more economical |
| Weighs less than 7.5 tonnes | You don't need a truck driving licence |
| White paintwork | Easy to fix promotional vinyls |

You must always listen to what your customers are saying about your product or service. Sometimes what they say will surprise or even offend you.

 **tip**

Recognise that what your customers see as the most important features are the most important features. Your business is there to meet your customers' needs, not your own.

 **example**

**William Wrigley**

In the 1880s William Wrigley started a business selling laundry soap. He was very proud of his soap, and to encourage people to buy it he gave away free chewing gum with every bar. The trouble was that, while people loved the gum, they were not particularly impressed with the soap. William then had three choices:

- improve the soap and stop messing about with promotional gifts;
- ditch the soap and sell chewing gum instead;
- soldier on regardless, for surely others would soon come to value his soap.

Of course, William took the second option and chewing gum can now be found stuck to pavements and bus seats the world over. He changed direction completely and made his fortune. He listened to his customers.

# 10 ways to make your business more memorable

Your business needs to have a clear identity and personality. The easier it is for people to remember your business, the more likely they are to buy from you. Here are ten ways to make sure that your business is easy to remember.

1   **A good name** – the perfect business name makes it obvious what you do and why you're better. For example, Prestige Home Improvements, Economy Car Hire.

2   **A strong image** – for those who remember images more easily than words, a strong visual identity is important. Think about the Virgin, Starbucks and Walls logos.

3   **Hands and faces** – we are 'hard-wired' to recognise and remember the human form. Prove this to yourself by thinking about Michelin and Dunlop. Both make tyres, but only one has a happy tyre man as its logo.

4   **Memorable mission** – when Toyota developed Lexus as their high-end brand they publicly shared their mission. It was simply to 'beat Benz'. Those two words tell you all you need to know about Toyota's aspiration.

5   **Offer choice** – too many options will confuse people and too few make it easy for them to say no. Always have two or three options that are clearly different. Large, medium or small.

6   **Compare** – people find familiar brands more comfortable than new ones. To tempt them away, you need to explain how you're different – for example, 'We make an English "Brie" cheese.'

7   **Keep in touch** – it sounds simple but few manage to do it well. If you can keep in touch with your customers, perhaps by providing information they value, they're more likely to remember you when they want to buy.

8   **Listen** – communication should be a two-way thing. Seek feedback and act on it. Create a customer club or network. A Facebook group costs nothing to set up and can grow beyond your customer base to include potential customers too.

9   **Reward** – people like to be rewarded. That's why coffee shops give you a loyalty card and stamp it each time you visit, making your tenth coffee a free one! How can you reward or recognise customer loyalty?

10  **Become the best** – finally, a good reputation is the best way to be remembered. Strive for excellence and people will always want to buy from you.

 **recap**

However good you are at what you do, people will soon forget. As well as being as memorable as possible, you also have to be as proactive as possible.

## Protecting your brand

Your brand is effectively your customer proposition. It is what customers perceive you are and do. It is also what they remember about you. The best way to protect your brand is to make sure you define it tightly and communicate it effectively to your target audience.

Often, names, images and other characteristics define the way you describe your brand. These can in some cases be legally protected. This is called intellectual property and is a potential legal minefield unless you are guided by an expert. Here are the basics.

● **Trade marks™** – anyone can put the ™ symbol next to their product name or logo. All it means is that the owner considers it to be a trade mark and wishes to make people aware of the fact. It costs nothing to do but affords limited protection from plagiarists.

● **Registered marks** ® – trade mark agents can help you register your brand names and logos. You can threaten to sue anyone who tries to copy you. The ® says this.

● **Copyright** © – the symbol means that the piece of work thus marked is the property of the author and cannot be reproduced without permission. Again it costs nothing to do.

● **Patent** – patent agents can work with you to protect a part of your product or process that is unique and specific to you. The registration process is lengthy and can be expensive.

**brilliant** **recap**

Often, the real value of a process or product you have created rests in your ability to prevent others from copying it. If you invent something new, you need to patent it. You will not get investors interested in an idea that is not protected.

# 10 design tips to bring what you do to life

Many of us 'think' in pictures and we are all strongly influenced by images – that's why advertising images can be so powerful. Your business, your product and the benefits you deliver will carry more weight if promoted using memorable images. You might decide to commission a graphic designer. Here are ten design tips to help.

1   **Pictures save words** – if you show people what it looks like, your words can then focus on explaining what it does. Think about those 'serving suggestion' photos on food packaging.

2   **Endorsements add weight** – persuade someone famous to endorse your product. Picture them on your promotional material.

3   **Sense of place** – the setting for photography is vital. Choose unusual locations that will appeal to your target audience and emphasise the benefits you offer.

4   **Simple messages** – your message has to be instantly obvious, wherever it is seen. Keep language simple and be explicit.

5   **Typography** – use a legible typeface and make the type big enough for everyone to read. Avoid using all capital letters and avoid white text on a coloured background – it's harder to read.

6   **Serifs** – these are the little tails that appear on characters in some typefaces. The experts say that serifs make text easier to read as they carry the eye from letter to letter.

7   **Colour counts** – green suggests environment, red aggression and blue cold. Look at ads for organic products, sports cars and refrigeration and you'll see examples. Choose colours that match your message.

8   **Consistency** – once you've got a logo or style, use it everywhere – letterheads, website, clothing and vehicles. It may seem contrived to you but it will build your brand.

9   **White space** – a single word in the centre of a blank page will create more impact than a page filled with information. Remember that less usually delivers more!

10  **Think customer** – your design work has to appeal to your customers, not you. Your taste is less important than your customers' expectation.

## The design brief

Before you seek the help of a graphic designer, make sure you have a really clear idea of what you want. Here are some questions a good designer will ask:

- What is the product or service you are offering and what does it do?
- How is it different from its competitors?
- Who buys it now? Describe your typical customer.
- Who do you want to reach and why?
- What do you want people to KNOW about:
  - your business?
  - your products or services?
  - your offer? (It can be good to create 'special offers' to raise interest.)
- What do you want people to THINK about:
  - benefits they'll gain?
  - value for money?
  - urgency – why is it important to buy now?
- What do you want people to DO:
  - visit a website?
  - give you a ring?
  - visit your outlet?
  - fill in and post a coupon?
- How much do you want to spend?
- What does success look like and how will you measure it?

### brilliant    tip

Use the headings above to write a clear design brief. It will save you time, frustration and ultimately money.

## Your website

Your prospective customers will expect to learn more from your website than they can from advertising or brochures. Your website must:

- form an integral part of your customer relationship;
- be easy to navigate with all the links working;
- provide as much in-depth technical information as people might need;
- be up to date with the latest news, prices and information;
- encourage people to identify themselves, perhaps by registering for regular updates.

**brilliant** recap

Your website can be your brochure, your catalogue, your archive, your shop and in fact your entire business. Amazon is a good example of a business that exists only online.

# 10 top marketing tips that experts rarely share

There are countless books on marketing theory. These tell you what and why but rarely how and when. Some of the best marketing tips are those developed by entrepreneurs themselves. Here are ten favourites.

1  **Free stuff** – a band gives away its latest track as a download. Fans have to provide their email address and postcode. The band can now organise gigs where most fans live and invite them to buy tickets.

2  **Omnibus** – new mums get a bag of baby products given to them in hospital. Mum is more likely to buy products that she's tried. The suppliers share the promotional cost.

3  **Cross-sell** – the zoo gives its visitors discount vouchers for the theme park and vice versa. Both know they'll only be visited once, so lose nothing by promoting each other.

4  **Classifieds** – these short lineage ads don't cost much to place, yet with the right words and a website can be powerful. For example, Find free marketing tips at **www.robertashton.co.uk**.

5  **Facebook ads** – social networking sites can allow you to target very accurately the people you want to see your ad. This means you can make very specific offers.

6  **Frequency** – regular small ads always work better than fewer big ones.

7  **Personalise** – the more personal your approach, the more likely your success. In other words, a tailored letter to a researched prospect will always do better than a blanket mailing.

8  **Specialise** – you can't supply all the people in the world wanting pet products but you can become an expert on say hamsters: **www.madabouthamsters.com**.

9  **Pre-booked visits** – one window cleaner books the next visit before he leaves and another waits for the phone to ring. Guess which has more work?

10  **Make it easy to say yes** – a low cost, no commitment 'starter pack' will make it easy for new customers to say yes and try you out.

 recap

Marketing theory is not to be sniffed at, but most of us simply want to know what will work for us. Try different things and measure the response. Become better at doing what works best for you.

 example

**Valerie Colling, Colling Construction, www.collingconstruction.co.uk**

Valerie first became interested in building when running a construction training company. She helped people who were out of work gain the skills, confidence and experience to work in the building industry. Because part of her work involved arranging work placements, she visited a lot of building sites and saw how reluctant many were to embrace new sustainable technologies.

An interest in 'green construction' and the knowledge that most established builders preferred traditional methods gave her the idea for Colling Construction. Research revealed a new technology, structural insulated panels, which are effectively factory-built walls and the next logical step on from timber-frame construction. Already proven in North America and Japan, Valerie decided to focus on bespoke homes using this very green technology.

To find her customers, Valerie became an expert contributor to a number of specialist websites, such as Restoration and Beyond, which attracts people interested in creating individual, environmentally sound character homes.

By being very specific about what she does and recognising that of the thousands of new homes built every year she only needs a handful to succeed, Valerie has made her business:

● specific − and clearly focused on one market niche;
● visible − by linking with advice websites visited by her target audience;
● accessible − by offering free advice to potential customers;
● realistic − knowing that she only needs a small market share to succeed.

## CHAPTER 12

# Succeed online

## Make more from your website

# 10 things the best websites have in common

As each year passes, it becomes more important for every business to be online. Every business needs a website. This can cost you a lot or a little, depending on what you want it to do. Here are ten things the best websites have in common – you might want your website to have them too.

1   **Easy to find** – you want your target audience to find your site. To do this, you must know who you're trying to reach and then make your site relevant to them. (Turn to the next checklist to learn about search engine optimisation.)

2   **Fast to download** – most people visit a business website for information, not entertainment. Avoid animation and graphics that take a while to download and play. Your visitor probably wants to go straight to the content.

3   **Compatible** – remember that there are several different web browsers. Things that work in Explorer™ may not appear the same in Firefox™. Some web designers forget this and simply design for their favourite web-browsing software.

4   **Easy to read** – use simple language and a design that makes it easy for people with poor vision. The charity RNIB has a useful guide at **www.rnib.org.uk**.

5   **Up to date** – keep adding new content and remove things that become out of date. Most content management systems enable you to set an expiry date on material you add.

6   **Free stuff** – make sure you have plenty of free stuff for people to read or download. Paradoxically, the more you give away, the more people will buy from you.

7   **Join up** – you want visitor feedback. You also want to build a list of prospects you can keep in touch with. Invite people to register for free regular newsletters and updates.

8   **Good links** – you don't have all the answers. Link to other sites that your audience will find helpful. Make sure they 'open in a new window'.

9   **Simple** – make sure that the visitor can navigate your site easily. Look at a few newspaper websites to see how common layouts make navigation almost intuitive.

10  **Silent** – singing avatars or striking music might appeal to you but could really annoy your website visitor. If sound is important to your message, make it optional!

## Getting the right website

It's usually worth using a professional web designer as, not surprisingly, this will give you a more professional result. Remember that for an increasing number of your customers your website is where they'll decide whether they want to do business with you or not.

Here are some things you need to consider and discuss when choosing a web designer.

- **Creativity** – can they present your message in an interesting, uncomplicated way?
- **Common sense** – are they practical and able to put themselves in your customers' shoes?
- **Experience** – have they created sites you like? Have they worked in your sector?
- **Content management** – you need to be able to add and edit content yourself. Get them to show you how this works before you commit yourself.
- **Evidence of success** – testimonials and a portfolio of good websites are important.

# 10 top search engine optimisation tips

Search engine optimisation is the process by which you encourage search engines to list your website before your rivals. If you can keep your site listed on the first page of a search, many more people will visit your website. Here are some basic tips to help you achieve this.

1    **Domain name** – the closer your domain name is to the search words your customers use, the better you will do. The best example is DIY store B&Q with **www.diy.com**.

2    **Multiple domains** – you can buy additional domain names quite cheaply, then 'point them' towards your website. This can help you have several generic domains.

3    **Key phrases** – the more your web copy repeats relevant key phrases, the higher it will be ranked. Clearly your text also has to make sense! It's no longer good enough to hide text that simply repeats the key phrase many times.

4    **Meta tags** – these are the words used to describe each web page in the html code. Although less important than they once were, most content-managed sites enable you to add these key words easily. Meta tags remain invisible on your website.

5    **Inbound links** – search engines look for links to your site from others as they are interpreted in some ways as endorsements.

6    **Reciprocal links** – avoid these as they are checked out by search engines and considered to be potential 'cheats'.

7    **Blog** – one good way to create inbound links is to create a blog, then insert links back from each blog to your website. Link to different pages on your site.

8    **Where you are** – if both you and your customers are mostly UK based, having a .co.uk domain will be better than using a .com.

9    **Site maps** – surprisingly, search engines use these to catalogue a site. Each page needs to be linked back to the site map.

10   **Words mean more than pictures** – search engines don't understand pictures. Make sure you add descriptive captions.

## Blogs

A blog is literally a 'web log' or online diary. They are easy to set up, using free sites like Blogger or WordPress. These sites let you create what is virtually a separate personalised website. You can add links, information, pictures and, of course, blogs.

Blogs enable you to:

● comment on current issues important in your business sector;

● invite feedback and prompt debate;

● link your blog to both your website and others.

Because of the high level of activity on blogging websites, stories posted are quickly picked up by the search engines. This means that people searching for information on a topic you've blogged about will find you. Note that journalists search blogs for comment; blogging can be good PR too!

 **example**

**Rob Greenland, www.thesocialbusiness.co.uk/blog/**

Rob is an activist-cum-social entrepreneur. He occasionally writes for the *Guardian* and writes a very good blog that attracts a lot of feedback. Rob's blog also wins him work, as a trainer and social enterprise adviser.

# 10 things to know before you sell online

It's nice to wake up every morning to find that people have been spending money on your website overnight. Here are ten ways to help you make this dream a reality.

1   **A good website** – it's obvious but needs stating anyway. People will only spend money via a website that inspires confidence and is clear, professional, accurate and up to date.

2   **Secure payments** – e-commerce means taking credit card payments. These need to be handled securely. Using PayPal to start with will cost you less than setting up a card merchant account with your bank.

3   **Try then buy** – you need to let your prospects see what it is you are selling. That's why many software companies let you download trial versions with a limited life.

4   **Simple products** – the easier your offer is to understand, the more likely people are to buy. Hotel accommodation, books, music and software are ideal for e-commerce.

5   **Specialise** – the smaller your niche market, the more likely it is that people will buy from you rather than look for cheaper rivals.

6   **Customer feedback** – encourage your customers to post comments and feedback on your website. Positive feedback reassures new customers. Act on negative feedback; thank the person who posted it and then remove it from the site!

7   **Affiliates** – it's quite easy these days to set up affiliate links to and from your site. This means that when your visitors follow links and then buy, you earn a small commission.

8   **Google™ advertisements** – you can pay to have your website appear when your chosen key words are put into the search engine. Google allows you to cap expenditure.

9   **Manage expectations** – only promise what you can do. Charge a premium for next day delivery.

10  **Keep in touch** – as with all customers, don't ignore them once they've purchased. Find new things to offer them to keep them spending. Offer incentives to encourage referrals too.

## E-commerce opportunities

Almost any business has the opportunity to engage in e-commerce. Not all opportunities are obvious, so here are some you might not have thought of.

- **E-books** – write down all those useful shortcuts you have discovered and add them to your website as downloadable pdf files. Sell lots of them at a low price.
- **Old stock** – create an online 'bargain basement' and use it to sell off stuff you want to get rid of. Include delivery in the price to make it really easy for people to buy.
- **Rare spares** – perhaps you have an interest in classic cars. Find suppliers of those hard-to-get parts and market them online. You sell, they dispatch and you make a profit.
- **Online advice** – if you really know your subject, people will pay to have you answer a question. You might even sell short consultations via online chat or Skype.
- **Photographs** – if you're a keen photographer, sell downloadable images.

## brilliant example

**Keith Milsom, www.AnythingLeftHanded.co.uk**

Keith's company supplies left-handed people with a wide range of things that make life easier. From scissors to pens, guitars to golf clubs and much more besides. The company was set up in 1968, trading from a shop and by mail order. Today all their business is done online.

As well as selling an amazing array of products, the website provides advice, information and video clips showing how to use many of the products. Customer feedback is encouraged and people soon feel they're part of a community.

The biggest reason for the company's success is simple. It focuses on meeting the individual needs of the 10 per cent of people who are left handed. If you're left handed yourself, you'll know what this means!

# 10 ways to build an audience

Having set up your website, you now want to attract as many visitors as possible. As well as search engine optimisation, you need to create as many opportunities as possible for people to discover then visit your website. You also want to know who those people are so you can keep in touch. Here are ten ways to build your audience.

1   **Capture details** – your website needs to encourage people to tell you a little about themselves. The more they tell you, the more specific you can make your offers to them.

2   **Facebook** – setting up a group or fan page on Facebook is a great way to build and interact with an audience. Add links from Facebook back to your website.

3   **Blogs** – not only is it good to have your own blog, but adding comments to popular blogs read by your customers will also encourage people back to your site.

4   **Amazon** – posting an Amazon review and using your website as your 'location' means that everyone reading the review can click through to your site. Make the review relevant to both the book and your business. Start by posting one for this book!

5   **Spam** – you can buy huge lists of email addresses and send them bulk emails. The response rate is usually very low but for some businesses it works.

6   **Press blogs** – most newspaper, magazine and trade journal websites usually invite readers to comment. Becoming active on the most relevant sites and subjects will push people to your site.

7   **People you already know** – get some cards printed that explain the benefits of being signed up on your website. Hand these to everyone you meet. Give them extra copies to pass on.

8   **Incentives** – offer people an incentive to register. The better the incentive, the wider word will spread.

9   **PR** – if your offer is strong enough, it might be newsworthy in itself.

10  **Events** – attend events, perhaps even speak at some, handing out fliers that encourage people to visit your website.

## Managing your audience

Building your audience is important, but once you have them you need to manage them. This might not be a problem at first, but as numbers build so too does the challenge. Actor Hugh Laurie has more than 700,000 fans on Facebook. How would you handle 10 per cent of that number?

Luckily there are a number of online databases you can subscribe to. A good example is **www.constantcontact.com**, which for a monthly subscription can:

● automatically list new subscribers who register via your website;

● enable you to group contacts according to interest or source;

● provide easy-to-use templates for email newsletters;

● enable you to build then send your e-newsletter;

● provide statistics to tell you who opened the email and what links they followed.

**brilliant** tip

When building your contacts database make sure you start out with a system that can handle one hundred times the number of people you're expecting to recruit. That way, you'll always be able to cope!

## CHAPTER 13

# Meet people

Network on and offline

# 10 top networking tips

Do you find networking daunting? Most of us find it difficult to approach and talk to complete strangers. Here are ten tips to help you get networking.

1   **Know what you want** – if you go networking with a clear goal, you'll be more focused. This means you'll talk to the right people and ask the right questions.

2   **Know what you do** – it can be surprisingly difficult to explain what you do. Have a prepared introduction. Be comfortable explaining who you are, what you do, why you're different and what you're seeking – in less than a minute.

3   **Volunteer** – whatever you join, become active. Having a role gives you good reason to talk to people. Offer to help organise the events you attend.

4   **Ask questions** – everybody likes to talk about themselves. Get people talking and then steer the conversation towards your areas of interest. Don't look bored.

5   **Look the part** – what you wear says a lot about you. Try not to dress like everybody else. Invest in the services of a good image consultant – the results can be amazing!

6   **Be memorable** – carry business cards and offer them freely. You want people to remember you when they get back to work. Also make sure you wear a name badge.

7   **Shake hands** – always greet people with a smile and a firm, but not too tight, handshake. Look them in the eye as you say 'hello' – you'll appear more confident.

8   **Eat first** – it's difficult to talk with your mouth full. Eat before you go and politely nibble rather than load your plate. You're there to network, not fill your belly.

9   **Move on** – don't spend the entire event with one person. To move on without seeming rude, touch their arm as you make your excuse to leave. However, only do this if it feels right to you.

10  **Take notes** – take a moment to record what you've said, heard or promised to do – otherwise you'll have forgotten by the following morning.

## Business networking clubs

Networking is rather like a bank savings account – you have to make several deposits before you can hope to earn interest and make a withdrawal. There are several business networking clubs you might consider joining. Some are specific to an area or industry while others form part of national and international networks. For example, if you joined the local branch of one of the large breakfast networking organisations, you would probably find:

- up to 50 people who meet on the same morning every week;
- no direct competitors, as most limit membership to one per business sector;
- an opportunity to talk every week about what you're looking for;
- regular opportunities to talk to the group about what you do;
- networking training sessions;
- members committed to introducing each other to new customers.

Online networks provide an almost overwhelming array of people you can network with. Most have a search facility to enable you to identify common interests, as well as various forums where you can debate pertinent issues.

In some cities you will also find professional networking facilitators. These are individuals or firms who arrange events at which people can meet each other. These are rather like dating agencies in the way that they work, except business is the objective rather than pleasure.

### brilliant example

**Brad Burton, 4 Networking, www.4networking.biz**

Brad Burton is something of an extrovert who loves networking. Having tried breakfast networking for himself, he decided to start his own breakfast networking organisation. One thing he's always disliked are rules, so he set up 4 Networking to be flexible. 'I wanted to focus on meeting member needs,' he explains, 'because satisfied customers means success for us too!'

Members are given a 4 Networking 'Passport' and are encouraged to visit other groups as well as support their own. In the first two years 4 Networking grew to more than 200 groups.

For you, networking will win you business; for Brad it is his business!

# 10 places to meet new people

Networking is all about meeting new people, but where? Being where your potential customers can be found is easier said than done. Here are ten places you might try. Some are less obvious than others!

1  **Exhibitions** – you don't have to exhibit to do business at a trade fair. Go where your potential customers are exhibiting and chat to them when the event is quiet.

2  **Networks** – business networks of all kinds can be a good source of new contacts.

3  **Conferences** – be seen at the events where new ideas in your business sector are being discussed. Prepare and ask challenging questions too – it gets you noticed.

4  **Where your customers gather** – if several of your customers use the same golf club, other members might be worth meeting too. Why not join and find out?

5  **Seminars** – what are the emerging topics of interest to your better customers? Attend seminars that explore them – or maybe even organise some yourself.

6  **Protest meetings** – if your customers are protesting about slow broadband, poor transport or a new wind-farm consider joining in – providing, that is, you agree with them!

7  **Reunions** – the chance to meet former school chums, college pals or one-time colleagues might result in some good business connections. Reunions can also be fun!

8  **Local schools** – if your business sells to families then get involved with the local school. Do something that helps the school and introduces you to parents. Don't try to sell; just make it easy for people to know what you do!

9  **Through volunteering** – lots of people have successfully broadened their network by volunteering. People who give their time tend to be more successful than those that don't.

10  **By making the news** – get yourself in the local or business press regularly and people will want to network with you.

## brilliant recap

People do business with people they know. So the more people who know you, the more new customers you are likely to meet. It really is a numbers game!

## Rules of networking

Do:

- make a point of trying to meet new people;
- become comfortable describing what you do;
- hand out business cards;
- encourage those you meet to introduce you to others;
- follow up any leads or introductions within 24 hours.

Do not:

- spend too much time networking – you have to work too!;
- complicate your elevator pitch – detail can come later;
- grab the attendance list and follow up everyone on it – you'll annoy people;
- try to sell to everyone you meet;
- forget to introduce those you meet to others you think can help them.

**brilliant** tip

**Three golden rules of networking**

- Listen more than you speak.
- Help others before expecting them to help you.
- Remember that shy people are often the most interesting – make an effort!

# 10 ways to network online

One of the internet's greatest strengths is its ability to connect people who otherwise would never find each other. This means you can seek out and find people to work with, buy from, sell to and even have a relationship with. Here are ten ways to network online.

1   **Blogs** – there are many websites where you can post blogs. Blogging is rather like keeping an online diary or journal. It's your chance to comment on what's happening. Make your blogs interesting and others will comment or make contact.

2   **Forums** – many websites have forum areas. These enable you to post questions and answer those that others have asked. The best forums are those with a very specific focus. You can pick up good tips and leads from forums read by people in your industry.

3   **User groups** – here you join a closed email 'special interest group' where you can email all members simultaneously. Again, the tighter the focus, the more relevant the exchanges. You usually have to apply to join a user group.

4   **Online communities** – there are many online business communities. One of the most popular is **www.ecademy.com**. Online communities enable you to publish your own profile and search for others using key words. Then you can email to make contact.

5   **Google alerts** – you can set these up from the Google homepage. Once confirmed you will receive an emailed link to any new web page that carries your search phrase. Set one up to let you know whenever your name is quoted anywhere on the internet.

6   **RSS** – many good websites provide an RSS feed. This simply means that you can sign up and receive notification whenever the site owner adds new content. Add an RSS feed to your own website and others will be able to see what's new without visiting the site.

7   **Subtle searching** – use search engines to find the people you'd like to meet, then email them to introduce yourself. Make sure that you make it clear what's in it for them. Don't hassle people – some will simply choose to ignore you, so just accept it.

8   **Diaries and databases** – if you're going to communicate with lots of people, you need to use appropriate software to help you remember what you've agreed to do.

9   **Being receptive** – networking is a two-way process. If people dig you out as part of their online networking, respond politely and be helpful. Help others and others will help you.

10 **Being aware** – in business, as in social networking, everything someone tells you may not be true. Wherever possible look for testimonials and endorsements to back up any claim.

You can waste an awful lot of time networking online. Many people may be keen to chat, but few will be willing to do business with you. Make a clear distinction in your mind between business and social networking. There is a time and a place for both, but when you're working focus on the business opportunities.

Most online networking communities charge a modest monthly subscription. In return you get greater functionality. Some offer access to 'inner circles' of contacts for a higher subscription. You need to be confident that these people will really be useful to you before you sign up.

## 80:20 rule

Every business textbook talks about the 80:20 rule. The phrase was coined by Pareto and suggests that 80 per cent of the profit comes from 20 per cent of the customers. It also applies to networking, in that 20 per cent of your network will deliver 80 per cent of the value you gain. Be selective.

### brilliant example

**Jenny Stockman, Framlingham Technology Centre, www.t-centre.co.uk**

Jenny co-founded a high-tech business centre in the heart of rural Suffolk. The centre is home to many of the area's most innovative companies. Most are small and all rely on networking to connect with customers and collaborators around the world. Some are even virtual tenants, buying administrative support and renting meeting rooms as and when they need them.

As well as attending networking events elsewhere, Jenny organises networking events at Framlingham Technology Centre. She brings to the centre speakers she has heard or met elsewhere, introducing them to her local business community.

One of the reasons that people choose to base their business here is that, despite being situated in a rural market town, it is a very busy enterprise hub. That's just one of the benefits Jenny gains from her business networking.

# 10 tips for Twitter and Facebook

Everyone is talking about the social networking revolution. It is certainly rev-olutionising the way we keep in touch with family and friends. In business the benefits are clear, but only if you focus on business. Here are ten ways to make online social networking work for you.

1   **You can't be everywhere** – every month more online networks emerge. Each is tempting in its way, but you don't have time to be active on them all. Choose no more than three.

2   **Remember Pareto** – only a small proportion of people on any online network are active. The audience you're reaching is probably smaller than you think.

3   **There are no secrets** – remember that stuff you post on sites like Facebook is going to be seen by anyone checking you out. It's a great opportunity to let people see your human side. Be you, but be sensible too!

4   **Link to your website** – add lots of hyperlinks back to your website. This makes it easy for people to click through. It also helps your search engine ranking;

5   **You're not Stephen Fry** – it's important to add frequent updates to Facebook and Twitter but be realistic. Stephen Fry's every move is eagerly awaited. Yours will be of less interest. Tweet what's relevant to those you want to influence.

6   **Comment counts** – your audience will be interested in what you think about the hot topic of the day. Comment and, if you can, provoke debate.

7   **Email links** – add your Facebook and Twitter links to your email signature. You want as many people as possible to find your social networking page.

8   **Ask questions** – many people will tell you that the biggest benefit of Twitter is that you can ask a difficult question and receive answers within minutes, often from people you don't know. Make sure you ask and answer questions.

9   **Watch competitors** – follow your rival on Twitter and become a Facebook fan too. This keeps you up to date with what they're doing. Are your competitors also follow-ing you?

10  **Survey opinion** – once you have a good online following you can easily and cheaply solicit people's views and opinions. Use sites such as Survey Monkey to build profes-sional surveys.

 **brilliant** tip

Don't neglect face-to-face networking because you find online networking more comfortable. For most people, both are equally important.

## Facebook – nuts and bolts

If you've not yet signed up with Facebook it's probably worth doing. Once you have a profile set up, you can:

● search for and link with people, businesses and causes you find interesting;

● set up groups of like-minded people;

● create your own fan page;

● create Facebook ads and be very specific about the profile of those you want to see them.

## Twitter – nuts and bolts

Twitter is more interactive than Facebook and can be confusing at first. Once you've created your profile you can:

● search for and follow people, businesses and causes you find interesting – this means that:

  ● you can (and should) post frequent, relevant 'tweets' (140 character messages);

  ● you automatically receive the 'tweets' of those you follow;

● use specialist free software to manage Twitter (for example Tweetdeck) – these make it easier to manage your network;

● include weblinks in your 'tweets', shortening them first using a site such as tinyurl.

## CHAPTER 14

# Get sales

How to win and keep
customers

# 10 ways to sell

The easier you make it for people to buy from you, the more you will sell. It sounds obvious, but there may be ways to sell that you have overlooked. Imagine you are a beekeeper. Here are ten different ways you could sell your honey.

1   **Retail** – perhaps you are a small-scale producer. Retail gives you the highest possible margin. You sell honey in your own shop or at the garden gate.

2   **Wholesale** – you have lots of bees and make more honey than you can sell through your own shop. You sell to other shops at a lower price and they sell on to their customers. You sell more but make less per jar. Your cost per jar falls so total profit grows.

3   **Through an agent** – every shop within range now stocks your honey. To get to shops further away you hire a sales agent. They represent a range of health food producers and take a commission on what they sell to their shop-owning customers. You get even less per jar, but you shift truckloads of honey.

4   **Online** – you list your honey on a busy health food website and set up a website of your own. You sell at your retail price with free postage. You no longer need your shop.

5   **Mail order** – you place ads in a cookery magazine and people send you cheques. You're selling your honey at full price, but you have to pay for the ads and hope that they work.

6   **By recommendation** – you offer your customers some of your new beeswax furniture polish if they introduce a friend who buys honey from your website.

7   **Through networking** – you join a breakfast networking group and put honey on all the tables. You encourage people to spread it on their toast. Many of them buy a jar and soon you're invited to lots more breakfast clubs.

8   **At an event** – last weekend you sold honey at a healthy living event. Tonight you're speaking to the Women's Institute. You have some small sample jars to hand out.

9   **Multilevel** – you ask your friends round and offer them commission if they can persuade their friends to sell your honey to people they know. Soon lots of people are selling your honey and you've started selling jam and marmalade too!

10  **As a package** – a budget hotel opens just down the road. They don't have a restaurant so you sell them breakfast packs containing bread and your honey.

## Choosing what's best for you

You probably don't sell honey, but you probably can adapt many of these different ways to sell to your own business. Much depends on the scale of your business. Bear in mind the following.

- Selling direct is best when:
    - you only need a few large orders;
    - your product or service is complex or bespoke;
    - you are trading locally where reputation is everything;
    - there are few alternatives so people have to come to you.
- Selling via others is best when:
    - you want to roll out your product quickly;
    - established distributor/retail networks already have the customers;
    - you prefer not to recruit a large number of salespeople;
    - your product adds more value when sold with something else.
- Selling online is best when:
    - your market is small, specialist and widely spread;
    - you are confident you can attract visitors to your website;
    - you want to sell to members of online networks and communities;
    - your product has a low unit cost and is easy to deliver.

**brilliant** **example**

**Alastair Sawday, www.sawdays.co.uk**

Alastair built a business publishing guides that list upmarket B&B accommodation. The guides are produced annually and are distributed via the book trade. Accommodation owners pay to be listed in his guides, although one of Alastair's inspectors visits first to make sure the accommodation is up to the high standards he knows his readers have come to expect.

The internet has revolutionised his business. You can now search his website for accommodation as well as purchase copies of his printed guides. While this has reduced sales through the book trade, it has been more than compensated for by his ability to list new accommodation as soon as it has been inspected.

By giving his customers a choice between printed guides and an interactive website, he has grown his total audience. His website also contains a blog where he shares his thoughts, and customers are encouraged to pay to join an exclusive Travel Club. This earns them discounts on books and accommodation.

By combining two routes to market, as well as by diversifying into new and emerging sectors such as ecotourism, the company has continued to grow and prosper.

# 10 top tips on closing more sales

Sales orders are the energy that fuels your business. But even when confronted by an interested new customer, you still have some work to do. Here are ten tips that will help you close more sales.

1　**Consider why you buy** – reflect on the things that encourage you to buy. What do you like salespeople to say to you? Do they show genuine interest? Learn by buying. (But don't spend too much!)

2　**Look** – watch salespeople in action. Exhibitions are great for this. In particular, look at how being too pushy usually drives the prospect away.

3　**Listen** – people will only give you the time of day if they have decided that what you are offering is interesting. Ask them what they want from you. Let them do the hard work!

4　**Know** – get to know your rivals' products or services inside out. Never knock them – simply focus on the differences that support your case.

5　**Deal with objections** – if the customer says no, ask them why and then deal with their concerns. Then ask for the order again.

6　**Care** – think of your prospects as human beings and not orders waiting to be placed. Show that your interest in them is genuine. Take the time to build rapport before seeking the order.

7　**Reassure** – build confidence in you and what you are selling. Be confident in yourself.

8　**Illustrate** – pictures can say more than words. Use pictures to show people how what you're selling can be used.

9　**Use testimonials** – collect positive feedback from past customers and use them to illustrate your presentation. They don't have to be high-profile past customers, just honest ones.

10　**Believe** – if you are passionate that you are offering the best option to your customers, you will succeed. If you're only after the cash it'll be much harder. You must believe.

You don't necessarily have to be well versed in the stages of the sale to succeed at selling. Sometimes the so-called professional salesperson comes over as being just a little too glib to be totally believable. In fact, some of the most successful salespeople don't conform at all. Instead, they win business because they know their industry, are passionate about their product and take the trouble to understand their customers. Enthusiasm and honesty outweigh manipulative techniques!

## brilliant recap

There is no secret to sales success. You just have to believe in yourself, believe in what you are selling and, above all else, believe that your customer will gain real value from the transaction you are hoping to do.

## Buying motives

A good way to think about how you are going to sell is to consider the reasons why people buy. A good mnemonic to help you remember is the word SPACED. Each letter represents a common reason for buying – what salespeople call a buying motive:

Security – is this safe and will it work?

Performance – will it meet my needs?

Appearance – does it look good? Will buying it make me look good?

Convenience – is it easy to introduce and use, or will it cause me problems?

Economical – can I afford to run it? How much will it save me?

Durability – will it last long enough for me to recoup the investment?

## brilliant example

**Jamie Mulhall, Mayday Office Systems, www.maydayoffice.co.uk**

Jamie started his sales careers selling office equipment and is now sales director of a successful and diverse office systems company. He remains one of the best photocopier salesmen in the business. He's very popular with his customers.

The secret of Jamie's success is that he always sees things from his customer's perspective. He takes the trouble to know what they will use his equipment

▶

for and how it can integrate within their existing systems. He even helps them calculate their current in-house printing costs and the cost saving his suggested solution can offer.

Jamie is good at selling because he makes it very easy for people to buy from him. He helps them to weigh up the pros and cons of what he is proposing. Only if they can convince themselves does he take their order.

# 10 benefits of selling through others

It is often tempting to try to sell direct and avoid sharing your profits with a distributor – in some sectors they demand a 50 per cent margin. However, distributors often have an existing relationship with your potential audience and can sell far higher volumes of your product or service than you can on your own. Here are ten valuable benefits that distributors can offer.

1   **Customers** – they are already supplying people with the potential to buy your product, otherwise why would they stock it? It's instant access to a warm, potential market.

2   **Knowledge** – builders, farmers and other merchants stock everyone's products. While unlikely to betray confidences, distributors can give you valuable product and pricing advice because they also sell for your rivals. They will tell you if you're too expensive.

3   **A shop window** – many distributors operate retail outlets. They can literally provide a shop window to display your products.

4   **Credit control** – by selling to distributors you reduce your risk of bad debt. The distributor has to collect payment from all their customers. You bill the distributor.

5   **Stockholding** – many will have warehousing and be prepared to take your product as you make it, reducing your need to store finished goods.

6   **Delivery** – by delivering your products at the same time as they deliver others, transport costs are lower than if you delivered direct yourself.

7   **Language** – if you want to sell overseas, working with a local distributor who understands the language and business culture is usually the only way.

8   **Credibility** – if you provide professional services, distributors and intermediaries can win you work by staking their reputation on your ability.

9   **Two bites** – you can have two bites from one market if you sell your distributors an 'own brand' version of your branded product. By offering choice you sell more.

10  **Feedback** – when testing new ideas your distributor's sales team can assess the market by simply discussing the idea with their customers.

Distributors, however, are not a panacea for all marketing challenges. In some sectors your distributors will want you to invest significantly in their marketing activity. Alternatively, they might only work for you if you can encourage new customers to come to them, which means consumer marketing. The key is to negotiate a 'business plan' with each distributor.

## Managing distributors

There is an art to managing distributors effectively. They must be motivated, informed and supported. Equally, they should not become so vital to your existence that they can call the shots. Here are five ingredients from which you and your distributors can create a recipe for success.

- **Agree targets** – the more considered and detailed the targets, the more you will both focus on achieving them. Product mix, pricing, sales per month and level of support can all be targeted and measured.
- **Product knowledge** – people only sell what they feel they understand. Provide literature and sales aids to help them to explain the benefits.
- **Incentives** – underpin key targets with incentives. These can be additional margins for the company or target-related rewards for their salespeople.
- **Review** – both sides should review progress against the targets regularly and discuss how to make up any shortfalls.
- **Campaigns** – short, sharp campaigns focusing on a single product or opportunity can get you a greater share of the distributor's attention for a short spell.

# 10 benefits of selling direct

Sometimes it makes more sense to sell direct to the user of your product or service. Perhaps you work as a one-man band and don't want to grow a big business. Here are ten benefits to selling direct.

1  **Few customers** – if you need only a small number of customers, as is often the case in a business-to-business environment, you're better to go and find them yourself.

2  **Relationships** – if you are providing a personal service – for example, as a life coach – people are buying *you*. You are the service and will win new customers because of it.

3  **You get referrals** – some businesses – for example home improvements – win almost all their new business from people introduced by satisfied customers. These are easier to get if you sell direct.

4  **You're in touch** – if you or your staff talk to customers, you get to hear pretty quickly if things in your marketplace change. You're not getting market feedback second hand.

5  **Control** – if you're someone who feels that no one else can do the job as well as you, then selling direct is your opportunity to prove this to yourself. Remember, it's your business and you must be happy with it.

6  **Specialist** – perhaps people will only buy from you because you have expert knowledge. If this is the case, get others to do everything else so you can just talk to customers.

7  **Loyalty** – if you hire and develop your own sales team they will spend all their time selling for you. No distributor can give you that level of commitment.

8  **Negotiate down** – you can be more flexible when selling direct. Distributors, quite rightly, need to refer back to you before deviating too far from your agreed trading terms. Sometimes it's right to 'have a deal' and get the order.

9  **Negotiate up** – everyone encounters opportunities to take an order at a higher margin. When your distributor does this they are unlikely to share the extra profit with you.

10  **Sell extras** – in some markets, once the order has been taken, you can add profitable extras to the deal. Remember, the most important thing about any sale is the total profit it generates for your business.

Recognising that your enthusiasm coupled with your belief in your product or service are the most important factors, it's useful to have a track to follow when you're making your sales presentation. Here are the stages most sales interviews go through.

- **Approach** – you need to get in front of your prospect. This means identifying people likely to be interested in what you have to offer and getting yourself in front of them.
- **Rapport** – tuning in to the same wavelength is vital. Good salespeople do this through their introduction and through showing an interest in the customer and their needs.
- **Probing** – by asking open questions (those that cannot be answered with yes or no) find out which issues you might be able to solve. By probing you can identify specific opportunities for your product or service. Your questioning directs the conversation.
- **Proposition** – having established what the need is, explain (or, better still, show) how your solution is the best. Use benefits (what it does) not features (what it is) to paint a positive picture in the mind of your potential customer. Value must outweigh the cost.
- **Closing** – having discussed how your solution is perhaps the right one, go for commitment – quite simply, ask for the order. Use closed questions (that can only be answered yes or no) to seek commitment.
- **Follow-up** – once you've got the order be sure to do what you have promised to the customer. Otherwise all the hard work will have been wasted.

The same process is used when phoning to arrange sales appointments. The difference is that you are selling the idea of a meeting, not your product or service.

 **tip**

Offering alternatives makes saying no more difficult – for example, 'Would you like us to deliver on Wednesday or Thursday?' 'Would you prefer it in blue or green?'

# 10 common sales pitfalls and how to avoid them

You won't get every sale you go for. Sometimes you've not got what the customer really needs, or it's the wrong time, or the customer cannot really afford what you're proposing. Here are some common pitfalls that might get between you and the success you deserve.

1   **Not listening** – you're so keen to tell your story you forget to listen to what your prospect has to say. The danger is that you tell them what they don't want to know and neglect to tell them what they do.

2   **Not closing** – your fear of being turned down means you don't ask for the order and lose your opportunity. It's only by trying to close that you discover the objections you need to overcome.

3   **Not knowing** – it really is vital that you prepare properly and can answer any questions that come your way. Going along unprepared is pointless.

4   **Not researching** – the internet means you can learn about the person and organisation you're meeting. Research means you can more accurately match their needs.

5   **The wrong person** – you're getting all the right enthusiastic vibes but the person just won't place the order. Usually this is because they're not the decision maker and need to ask someone else.

6   **No budget** – you get the order easily but find it a real problem getting paid. You realise they only gave you the order because no one else will supply them. If a deal seems too good to be true, it probably is!

7   **Too cheap** – if you don't know your costs, it's easy to be talked into selling too cheap. Always offer more for the same price as an alternative to reducing your price.

8   **Being critical** – criticise what someone's doing at the moment and you criticise them. Say why your offer is better, not why what they're using now is worse.

9   **Assuming intimacy** – you can have a long and successful business relationship with someone and never really know your buyer as a person. Respect their privacy and don't interpret friendliness as wanting to become your friend.

10  **Not following up** – if you leave a sales meeting having promised to do something, do it! There's nothing worse than not following up. Your new customer will think you have lost interest.

 **recap**

The paradox is, the cheaper the deal, the more difficult the customer will become.

## Why sometimes it's best to walk away from a deal

We all have different perceptions of value. Think about when you go out to eat. Some people prefer a pizza chain and others a Michelin-starred restaurant. Both can stop you feeling hungry. You might agree that both have their appeal. One is better for a meal after you've been to the cinema and the other for a special occasion.

The problem comes when the Michelin-starred restaurant tries to compete on price with the pizza restaurant. Is that realistic? Probably not, but just suppose it tried. Here are some possible outcomes.

● A customer wanted a fast meal and becomes frustrated by the slower service you get in a gourmet restaurant.

● A customer is unsure about the food, being used to something more basic, and sends it back to the kitchen because the meat is 'undercooked'.

Both customers will feel hard done by as the restaurant tried too hard to meet their price expectation but did not deliver what they wanted. In other words, if a customer cannot see the value in what you are selling, they are probably not the right customer!

## CHAPTER 15

# Build a team

Recruit and manage people

# 10 questions to ask when recruiting

Without good people your business cannot grow. Recruiting the right people is vital to your continued success. Here are ten questions you might like to ask potential recruits when interviewing.

1   **Talk me through your career to date** – listen for and explore any gaps.

2   **What have been your greatest achievements?** – find out the highlights of the candidate's career so far. What are they proudest of having done and why?

3   **What has been your biggest mistake?** – making mistakes is how we all learn, so the more the better, within reason! Assure candidates that this is not a trick question.

4   **How do you want to be spending your time in three years' time?** – this reveals where they see their career going. Do you want an ambitious person or someone to stick at one job? The answer to that one rests with you.

5   **What appeals most about working here?** – this question reveals how much research they've done for the interview. Good candidates will have done their homework.

6   **What appeals least about working here?** – do they trust you enough to tell you? If not, have you failed to make them feel at ease with you? You will learn from honest answers.

7   **If you won £1 million tomorrow, how would you spend it?** – good to know what your candidate dreams of doing. How will working for you take them closer to that dream?

8   **What is the question you would most like to ask me?** – if you've established a good rapport the answer to this may reveal their concerns about your organisation.

9   **What is the question you hope I don't ask you?** – this encourages them to reveal fears and doubts about their ability to do the job. Respect them for what they are and reassure them.

10  **When I'm making my decision, what do you most want me to remember about you?** – this encourages them to summarise the key benefits they bring.

**brilliant** tip

Ask each candidate the same questions. This is both fairer on them and makes it easier for you to compare. Structure helps you recruit the best person for the job.

Before you start looking for people to interview:

- define the job clearly – how does it fit within your organisation and plans?;
- write a job description;
- check out what the going rate of pay is for similar jobs – you might decide to pay more;
- work out the total cost of hiring someone – include everything, even training;
- calculate the financial return on this investment – make sure they'll make you money.

You can find potential new employees by:

- advertising in local, national or trade publications;
- advertising online – using the recruitment website most likely to be visited by those you want to recruit;
- putting a sign outside your door;
- asking existing employees who they know;
- asking customers who they can recommend;
- networking;
- using a recruitment agency.

Job advertisements should always contain:

- the job title;
- the salary range and benefits;
- your contact details;
- a promise of confidentiality;
- positive reasons for joining your firm.

When interviewing:

- do not face the candidate over your desk – it creates a power inequality;
- if you work from home, interview at a local hotel – it will be more professional;

- listen more than you talk – this is vital if you are to understand the candidate fully;

- take notes and ideally get someone you trust to sit in to give a second opinion;

- smile – an interview can be daunting for both of you so keep it light and informal;

- offer to reimburse travel expenses;

- say thank you at the end and ask for feedback on the interview.

**brilliant** tip

However sure you are, never offer anyone the job at interview. Give both of you an opportunity to reflect. If you're really convinced, ring them later the same day.

# 10 positive ways to deal with employment legislation

Hiring someone is a big responsibility. You want to do the right thing, but the amount of legislation you need to comply with is daunting. Here are some things to consider to make sure you deal with the legal side of employment objectively.

1   **Balance** – remember that despite common opinion, employment law is there to protect you as well as your employees. Many doubt this, but it is true.

2   **Fairness** – if you are always fair, open and honest with your employees, they'll be far less likely to invoke the letter of employment law in a damaging way. Treat people badly and no amount of paperwork will give you the protection you need.

3   **Problem people** – there are people who make a career out of making claims against their employers. This is a particular problem in the public sector. Take references when hiring and hopefully you'll avoid hiring problem people.

4   **Common sense** – most of the legislation you will encounter does little more than underpin common sense. Use common sense and you won't go too far wrong.

5   **Don't discriminate** – it is illegal to use any selection criteria other than ability to do the job. In fact, shortlist with an open mind and you'll often be pleasantly surprised at interview.

6   **Delegate** – you don't have to deal with legislation yourself. Have a trusted team member handle it for you, or outsource to a freelance HR professional.

7   **Insurance** – make sure you have the right insurances to protect you and your staff. Remember that this also means their personal motor insurance if they make business journeys in their own car.

8   **Assess risk** – make an objective assessment of the various risks your employees face. Make sure you invest the most effort in protecting against the biggest risks.

9   **Keep up to date** – spend some time each year making sure you are still compliant. Rules change and you want to avoid getting caught out.

10  **Get help** – if you find yourself with an employment law problem, get professional help. Delay or DIY can both make the problem worse, not better.

## Employment contract

This is the agreement that exists between you as an employer and your employees. It does not have to be in writing although ideally it will be. As a minimum, you have to provide a written statement setting out the main points within the first two months of employment.

There are plenty of places online where you can find sample employment contracts. Many are complex and cover every possible eventuality. In a small business, the contract is usually contained within the letter that offers the job.

When you take on your first employee it's worth getting an employment lawyer or HR specialist to write you an employment contract that meets the needs of your business. This means it can be most specific about what's most important to you.

 **example**

**Elaine Pennell, Commercial Hub HR, www.commercial-hub.co.uk**

Elaine started her business in 2007 when she realised that too many small businesses only take HR seriously when confronted with an employment tribunal hearing. As she explained, 'When you get to tribunal the damage is already done. Not only have you got a very aggrieved employee but everyone else is probably feeling unsettled too.'

Elaine's company provides her clients with the kind of professional HR support they need, as and when they need it, so that they can avoid making costly mistakes.

# 10 things that will make you a better boss

It's almost a cliché but it can never be said too many times – your people are the biggest investment your business will ever make. For most businesses the wage bill is the biggest monthly cost. Here are ten ways you can become a better boss.

1   **Big ears** – good bosses not only listen, they also take a genuine interest in their staff.

2   **Long legs** – be seen to be interested and involved. Walk around the place – be seen.

3   **White teeth** – smiling bosses make people happy. Don't be grumpy as it can spread!

4   **Dirty hands** – in most small businesses there are always grotty jobs like unblocking toilets. Show that you're prepared to get your hands dirty.

5   **An open door** – at times you need to be left alone. Not everything you do can be shared, but being accessible is the best way to know what's happening.

6   **Clear vision** – people follow leaders who know where they're going and who don't falter.

7   **Tongue control** – emotional responses such as shouting and ranting have their place, but not if it means humiliating your staff. Sometimes it's best to hold your tongue.

8   **Strong stomach** – remember how officers led their men to certain death in the battles of the Somme? Like all the best leaders, if it's getting tough, you must not let your fear show.

9   **Firm hand** – you are the boss. You are expected to make unpopular decisions where necessary and to be firm with those who don't pull their weight. Don't be too soft.

10  **Love** – we are all human. We all like to be loved – good bosses show true love and compassion. Being heartless and brutal will not make you rich.

It may sound idealistic to be a touchy-feely, caring employer when the bank has a charge over your house and things aren't going as well as you'd hoped. However, being a great boss need not cost you the earth. Here are a few very affordable ways to make your business a great place to work.

- **Soft loo paper** – pay the extra few pence for the good stuff. Also make sure the toilets are clean and in good working order.

- **Graffiti board** – why not create places for your staff to have their say, free from criticism or retribution?

- **Good tools** – usually the best tools cost less than the wrong tools and waste less time.

- **Party** – investing £10 per head in a visit to the pub after work on a Friday can deliver hundreds of pounds' worth of extra work the following week.

- **Surprises** – we all like nice surprises – for example, ice creams all round on a hot day.

## brilliant example

**Henry Stewart, Happy, www.happy-people.co.uk**

Henry set up Happy Computers in 1990. His business was computer training and his vision to create a great place to work, both for his staff and his customers. Over the past 20 years the company has won many awards for being the best for customer service, great to work for and excellent at getting the right work/life balance.

'Imagine a company based around the principle that "people work best when they feel good about themselves"', explains Henry. 'Imagine a workplace where, instead of levels of approval, people are trusted to make the key decisions for themselves. Imagine trusting people to work out their own balance of life and work. Imagine a blame-free culture where mistakes are celebrated. Wouldn't you want to work there? We are still learning but that is the type of company we are seeking to create.'

How can you make your business happy too?

# 10 ways to delegate and share the work

Letting go of the stuff you used to do is the only way to grow your organisation. As the headcount rises your job becomes more strategic. You must now let others do the day-to-day tasks. Remember that you may be able to do their jobs but they can't do yours. Here are ten tips on delegation.

1   **Explain** – tell people exactly what you want done and why it's important.

2   **Invest** – spend time and money making sure everyone has the right equipment and skills.

3   **Encourage innovation** – the way you used to do it may not be the best way today. Encouraging others might lead to new and better ways to get things done.

4   **Allow mistakes** – it won't always be right first time. Accept a few mistakes.

5   **Allow routine** – let operational things become a series of routines. You might prefer every day to be an adventure but your staff probably would not.

6   **Empower** – make people responsible. Give them scope to be flexible and to adapt. Let them make the job their own.

7   **Don't interfere** – having delegated, the worst thing you can do is interfere. Wait to be asked for help. Create systems that enable you to monitor what's going on.

8   **'Morning prayers'** – lots of teams start the day with a 20-minute briefing. It allows everyone to know what's new, different or urgent. Do it standing up. Make it fun.

9   **Explore new things** – if you can delegate all your tasks you are not redundant. You now have time to dedicate to planning for the future.

10  **Celebrate** – create milestones and celebrate with the team when they are reached.

## Delegating in a social enterprise

In general, people who work for social enterprises are more passionate, idealistic and enthusiastic than workers in the 'for profit' sector. However, this can make them prone to believing that the vision they have for the organisation is better than yours. You can manage this by:

● involving your team in developing the strategy you want them to follow;

● collecting and then discussing feedback from customers and service users;

- accepting that you won't be right all the time – don't suppress good ideas;
- helping everyone to stay abreast of the current debates in your sector.

## Getting strategic

So you've delegated and now have more time on your hands. Here are five things you could do tomorrow that you didn't have time to consider today.

- **Clear** your desk of clutter, put your feet up and reread your business plan.
- **Visit** your five best customers and find out how you could both be more successful.
- **Research** and try to understand your competitors better.
- **Take time out,** relax and think about where you want your organisation to go.
- **Book a surprise** weekend away and treat your family to your attention.

**CHAPTER 16**

# Be motivating

Get the best from yourself
and others

# 10 ways to motivate yourself

Running your own business does not mean you are always going to feel motivated. At times, the tasks will seem too daunting and distractions will be too tempting. What's more, no one else is going to motivate you if you're the boss. Here's how to motivate yourself.

1   **Set daily goals** – if you plan what you want to get done each day, you're less likely to feel overwhelmed by your workload. Set realistic daily work goals.

2   **Treat yourself** – just as you plan what you're going to do each day, also plan how you will celebrate having completed those tasks. Small daily treats are good.

3   **Stay fit** – everyone knows that if you're physically fit you feel better and have more stamina. Schedule time for keeping fit – even if it's just a brisk walk at lunchtime.

4   **Share with a friend** – do you have a buddy who is also in business? Give each other permission to nag and check that tasks are being finished on time.

5   **See the big picture** – today might be tough, but view it as a step towards your ultimate goal. Thinking about the gain will reduce the pain.

6   **Be positive** – make the effort to see the positive in everything. No matter what the world throws at you, there's always a positive side. Find it and hold on to it.

7   **Pace yourself** – if enterprise was easy, we'd all be doing it! Success takes time, so accept that growing your business will not be straightforward. Read about how many of today's most successful people found life tough in their early entrepreneurial days.

8   **Limit surfing** – it's too easy to get distracted by the internet. Business networking sites can eat into your working day if you visit them too frequently. Avoid online chats with others who should also be working!

9   **Be tidy** – clutter can itself be demotivating. Keep your desk clear of all but the current challenges and tasks. If stuff doesn't get looked at for a week, file it or bin it.

10  **Be honest with yourself** – we're not all going to make millions and attempting the impossible can be frankly rather depressing. Be honest about what is possible for you and don't be unrealistically ambitious.

## Determination

As well as being self-motivated you need to be determined. People will always tell you (often with the best of intentions) that you are being too ambitious. Only you can decide if your plans are achievable. It's easy to give up but much more satisfying to prove the sceptics wrong.

Some of the world's most successful entrepreneurs succeeded because they were determined and single-minded. The more people told them they'd fail, the more determined they became.

Here are some examples.

- Sir Richard Branson set up Virgin Atlantic to compete with British Airways and succeeded in reducing the cost of transatlantic flights.
- Paula Radcliffe is a world class distance runner. Her determination to win by the rules and her abhorrence of the use of performance enhancing drugs drives her to excel.
- Fashion designer Mary Quant is credited with having created the miniskirt. Despite opposition from traditionalists she argued that the miniskirt was liberating. Media opposition boosted her determination to succeed.

 **tip**

Determination doesn't just help you succeed in business – it helps you succeed in everything you do.

**brilliant example**

**Brian Crosby, West End Gallery**

Brian is a talented artist with a temperament to match. His former wife pushed him into a teaching career which he found he really hated. He decided instead to open a gallery and picture-framing business in Cheltenham and later in Gloucester.

Competition was tough and his now ex-wife less than complimentary. Despite many setbacks, including staffing problems and cash flow problems, Brian is still trading. He's never going to become world famous, but his determination means he is going to spend his life doing work he enjoys.

# 10 things to do that will make you more motivating

Motivating yourself can be tough, but motivating others can be a far larger challenge. In fact, motivating those you employ can in itself be very motivating for you. Here are ten small things you can do that will make your staff happier at work. Happiness is a vital precursor to motivation!

1   **Make it bright and light** – banish brown paint and dirty windows. Make the work environment light and comfortable. Why not use some comfy sofas for meetings instead of hard chairs?

2   **Keep it clean** – nobody likes to come into work and find the bin full and the toilets smelly. Invest in a good cleaner and everyone will be much happier.

3   **Be flexible** – why not let people start early and go home early in the summer? Consider an annualised-hours scheme, which makes it easier to manage both your workload and their work/life balance. This can also make your business much more responsive.

4   **Celebrate together** – birthdays, new business wins and even Fridays can be good reasons to buy cakes for everyone.

5   **Provide nice drinks** – it's amazing how awful some cheap coffees taste. Treat people to decent drinks at work and don't make them pay. Ask people what they'd like and stock it.

6   **Create competitions** – lighthearted prizes for hitting targets make winning part of your workplace culture. Design some competitions to be won by junior team members.

7   **Organise outings** – do your staff work in the same place all the time? Take them out to meet customers, to hear relevant speakers and see things that will shape their work.

8   **Encourage sports** – encourage fitness by subsidising gym membership. People who are fit tend to enjoy better health and take less sick leave. Gym membership can be a good investment.

9   **Support their cause** – everyone has a cause they feel strongly about. Your staff will welcome your taking an interest, and perhaps even helping them out.

10   **Offer alternatives** – remember that while some people are extrovert, others are shy. Be careful not to create a culture where people feel obliged to take part in things they'd rather miss.

## Rewards packages

Everyone is different. Many large employers provide a flexible range of employment benefits from which employees can select. This enables people to be rewarded in the way that best suits their individual needs. It's actually quite easy for small organisations to offer flexible rewards packages too. Here's how to do it.

● Ask your team for comments and ideas.

● Cost those ideas, plus others you feel might be valued or welcomed.

● Make sure you are providing everything the law says you should.

● Take professional advice if you're worried or not sure about any aspect.

● Negotiate individual rewards packages with your team.

 **example**

### Virgin

Several years ago, one of the Virgin companies took over a building that used to be occupied by part of the civil service. It is a modern, open-plan building with lots of architectural glass and steel. Despite that, it was not an inspiring place, with grey walls, blue carpets and paper everywhere.

Virgin changed all that. Bright paintwork, large murals, a staff cafeteria and informal meeting areas transformed what had for years been a dull workplace into somewhere that people wanted to be.

How can you make your workplace somewhere people want to go?

 **tip**

### Individuality

The key to motivating people is to create and sustain a culture where they feel valued, recognised and properly rewarded. You must also give people the opportunity to retain their individuality in the workplace. Take the trouble to discover and understand how race, faith and other personal factors need to be accommodated.

# 10 training opportunities most overlooked

Training and personal development can make a tremendous difference to the way people perform in their jobs. Don't forget that this also applies to you as the boss. However, if you thought that training had to involve spending lots of money, think again. Here are ten low cost options.

1  **Share** – if you're a small business, club together with others to organise training sessions. It will cost less and be more convenient than buying places on open courses.

2  **Ask suppliers** – they gain if you become more proficient. See if they have spare places on in-house training programmes that your people can attend.

3  **Teach each other** – the best training happens in the workplace with your own experts helping others catch up. Because this can happen spontaneously it's often overlooked.

4  **Work experience** – supervising students who visit you to gain work experience will develop the supervisory skills of those who do not usually manage people.

5  **Become a school governor** – becoming a school governor provides excellent free management training. It makes people more objective in their own work.

6  **Become a charity trustee** – becoming a trustee enables people to develop their particular skill (for example, finance, HR or marketing) in a different context.

7  **Become a non-exec director** – if you work in the voluntary sector, why not become a non-executive director of a 'for profit' enterprise? Bring social awareness and learn about profitability.

8  **Grants** – there are many organisations able to give you training grants or provide free training. Look at local economic development websites.

9  **Read books** – some people find it easy to learn from books. Set up a company library – include training software and reward people who take items home to develop their skills.

10  **Online** – the internet is packed with learning opportunities. There are online training courses and web seminars you can attend virtually, and more.

To work out your organisation's training needs, it's important to compare the skills you have with those your mission requires. Different organisations have different needs.

To map out the skills in your team, you need to build a simple matrix with 'skills' on one axis and your team members on the other (see below). Compare this with your operational needs and you begin to see where there are gaps. Aim not to be reliant on any one person for a particular skill.

|         | Word | Excel | Sales | French | German | Spanish |
|---------|------|-------|-------|--------|--------|---------|
| Judith  | ✓    | ✓     |       | ✓      |        |         |
| Michael | ✓    |       | ✓     |        |        | ✓       |
| Tom     | ✓    | ✓     |       |        |        |         |
| Ruth    |      |       | ✓     | ✓      | ✓      | ✓       |

It is also useful to assess the level of ability in each area. This enables you to encourage the experts to spend time developing the abilities of those who are less skilled.

Try also to identify skills within your team that are not currently needed by the organisation. They may become useful in the future.

 **brilliant**   recap

There are many training opportunities for you and your team. Unless you point out that they have training value, people will not see them as training.

# 10 common people problems and how to solve them

Employing people can be one of the most rewarding things you do, but it can also be very frustrating. People, unlike machines, do not always behave consistently. There are many problems you can encounter as a boss. Here are some tips for dealing with ten common ones.

1   **Poor performance** – before complaining, take time to find out how your employee views their performance. Do they have a problem outside work? Do they need training?

2   **Poor timekeeping** – childcare, public transport and body clock can all impact on timekeeping. Many organisations offer flexible working – could you?

3   **Wrong person** – we all make mistakes and hire the wrong person. Accept that this is probably as much your fault as theirs – take professional advice and sort it out quickly.

4   **Poor health** – as long as someone is not shirking, you need to be sympathetic. Consider sickness insurance which can replace the pay of someone who is long-term sick.

5   **Neurotic person** – stress at work is a growing problem and some people are naturally neurotic. Make sure you know the difference between goal setting and 'dumping' on people.

6   **Romance** – many people marry someone they meet at work. Office romances are part of life. Be ready with the tissues if it all goes wrong. Never take sides.

7   **Private calls** – agree some ground rules for private phone calls, either on your phone or their mobiles. If you want people to work long hours, accept that they'll need to organise their lives too.

8   **Theft** – any criminal activity should be dealt with quickly. Take advice – cover-ups and quick departures do not set a good example to others. Accept that you may be the last to know that something is going on.

9   **Tragedy** – people die, become disabled, divorce; they get mugged, robbed, raped and tragically attacked. Your role as employer is to listen and support. Help people when they're down and they'll help you more when they're up again.

10  **You** – on reflection, many people problems are symptoms of poor management. Before roaming round the workplace lopping off heads, look in the mirror and make sure you're not the problem!

## Other things that can go wrong

Here are some tips on handling other things that might go wrong.

- **Accidents at work** – if someone is injured at work, you could face a heavy fine if faulty equipment or poor workplace practice was the cause. When accidents happen, sort out the emergency and then investigate fully. Be sure to inform your insurer. Cooperate with any outside agencies that get involved. Be prepared to face the media.

- **Accidents somewhere else** – yes, it can be worse. Road accidents involving your vehicles and industrial accidents involving the use of your products may be largely avoidable, but they do happen. Make sure you're fully insured and have a plan to fall back on.

- **Weather, war, etc.** – sometimes things happen that you cannot possibly predict or be prepared for. Europe learned in 2010 that volcanoes can ground a nation's planes. If the world looks like it's dealing you a rough hand, try to remain pragmatic and positive. Life's just like that sometimes.

## Ways to be prepared

It pays to be prepared in case things do go wrong. Here are some ways to be prepared.

- **Insurance** – the more remote the risk, the lower the premium and the more devastating it can be if it happens. Get insured.

- **First aiders** – make sure you have qualified first aiders in your team. Also make sure that vehicles and workplaces have first-aid kits and fire extinguishers.

- **Fire drills** – practise evacuating the building regularly. Avoid this when it's raining!

- **Security** – invest in good security alarms, lights, etc. Get them maintained regularly.

# 10 ways to manage stress in yourself and others

Running any kind of organisation can be pretty unforgiving. It's not surprising that stress is a common, though rarely talked about, problem. The truth is that as you grow your enterprise, you also grow yourself – that's one reason it can become stressful. Here are ten common signs of stress and some advice on how to cope with them:

1  **Frequent headaches** – if you are reaching for the aspirin, almost without thinking, it might mean that you're doing too much. Get some fresh air and reflect on your day.

2  **Butterflies** – these are important if you are to perform well in important meetings, but if you're stressed you may be feeling them far more often. Try to keep work in perspective.

3  **Self-medicating** – increasing consumption of coffee, alcohol, nicotine and even sugar can be signs of stress. Be aware of your consumption and what it might be telling you.

4  **Overreacting** – you fly off the handle when really the issue is not that important. Switching off seems difficult and everything's coming at you too quickly.

5  **Paranoia** – you are beginning to feel oppressed. Is the world really plotting your downfall? Or are you imagining the worst? Step back and try to be objective.

6  **In bed** – you might notice that two things are more difficult to manage. One is sleep and the other is your libido! Both are classic symptoms of stress.

7  **Digestive problems** – from indigestion to irritable bowel, your guts act as a barometer of your mood. Stress can cause digestive problems. Treat the cause and the symptoms.

8  **Poor judgement** – if you are stressed then your ability to make decisions is hampered. The consequences can be stressful in themselves. Try to defer big decisions or involve others.

9  **Escapism** – when severely stressed, facing work can be difficult. If you feel the urge to take time off, or even run away, seek professional help.

10  **Criticism** – if you work with other people they'll notice you becoming more stressed. They'll probably also be astute enough to identify the cause. Be brave and ask them.

Many of the physical symptoms of stress occur in response to the production of adrenaline, perhaps compounded by your intake of caffeine, tobacco and alcohol. While we all have panic attacks from time to time (and that's a normal part of business life), stress is something different. Stress levels can rise gradually so that you hardly notice the change. The result is that your effectiveness suffers and you become less user friendly. Both make it harder to achieve the goals you set yourself.

There are countless books, websites and other sources of advice dealing with stress. To get you started, here are a few tips that can help you avoid becoming unduly stressed.

- **Be realistic** – set out to perform well but do not be overambitious or set unrealistic goals.
- **Prioritise** – do today what has to be done today. Delegate as much as you are able and don't fret about tomorrow's task today.
- **Exercise** – however busy you are, make time for regular physical exercise in your working week. Exercising also provides good thinking time.
- **Share** – we all need a confidant, someone you know you can discuss things with openly who will be supportive and help you see things as they really are. Get a mentor.
- **Measure** – measure out the business journey and highlight the milestones. Measure progress all the time so that you can see what you've achieved as well as what's pressing.

## brilliant recap

We all need some stress to function. If you're too laid back nothing gets done. Too much stress though can literally kill you!

## Getting help

If stress is a problem then seek help. A search of the internet or local telephone directory will point you towards:

- charities that provide counselling and support for stress and mental illness;
- professionals (such as psychotherapists) who, for a fee, will help you unpick and resolve the issue;
- gyms where you can work out your stress and take time out.

Unresolved stress can damage your health, both physically and mentally. Don't let it!

CHAPTER 17

# Avoid surprises

Predict and overcome those
unexpected hurdles

# 10 staff surprises

It's true to say that taking on your first employee is one of the most demanding steps you have to take as you grow a business. Employees enable you to scale up your business to a point where, ultimately, it won't need you at all. For many, that is the ultimate goal. Here are ten staff surprises to look out for.

1  **Coming in late every day** – what's changed at home to make mornings difficult? Partying every night? Find out and offer to help. Pre-empt the problem.

2  **Gone shoppping** – has your employee combined a business trip with an afternoon at the shops? If they work hard and are committed, then turn a blind eye.

3  **Pilfering** – always make it clear what you consider to be reasonable in this respect. This is more of an issue in a sweet shop than a steelworks. Don't make rules and then break them yourself.

4  **Fraud** – if someone's robbing you or your business, call the police. Never compromise.

5  **BO** – it sounds trivial but a worker with a personal hygiene problem is one of the stickiest issues most bosses have to face. Encourage workforce peers to hint or help.

6  **Moonlighting** – some specialists – for example, graphic designers – take it as read that they can work for you in the day and themselves in the evening. Make your policy clear when you hire people. Avoid misunderstanding by setting out the deal at the outset.

7  **Overfamiliarity** – as your business grows, so too must the distance between you and your staff. There will simply be more things you cannot share. Manage the growing gap.

8  **Sickies** – it's always useful to record sick leave and check for patterns. Is it on the increase? Better to be asked for time off for personal matters than to have them ring in 'sick'!

9  **Different values** – we all have to be tolerant of the views of employees. But when every last yoghurt carton has to be recycled and skimmed organic milk is all they will put in their fair trade coffee, your tolerance might be challenged. Negotiate a fair compromise.

10  **Faith** – we live in a multicultural society and some people will decide not to undertake certain duties for religious reasons. Respect faith requirements and adapt accordingly.

Employment tribunals await those accused of discriminating against their employees. The fact is that when things go 'legal' everyone loses out. Negative publicity, workplace tension and the hassle and frustration of the process can all cause lasting damage to your business.

The art of avoiding workplace conflict is to prevent its ever happening. You can do this by:

- taking up references before you hire someone, however convinced you are;
- encouraging them to tell you about their values at interview;
- trusting your instincts;
- setting out the ground rules in a concise employee handbook;
- having professionally written contracts of employment.

If your business operates in a particularly sensitive area – for example, medical research or meat production – you need to make doubly sure that you have every angle covered before you hire staff. It is not unknown for journalists to pose as workers and then expose what they present as bad practices.

## brilliant    example

### Pendle Citizens Advice Bureau

Funding problems led this charity to make one of its management team redundant in 2008. The manager claimed he had been unfairly dismissed, saying he had been the victim of an 18-month campaign of bullying and intimidation because he was a 'whistle blower'.

It was April 2010 before the case came before an industrial tribunal. They found that the employer had not followed 'correct procedures' and therefore the employee had been unfairly dismissed. However, they also found that the employee had 'effectively contributed to his own demise by continually criticising senior staff'. No compensation award was made.

The long wait for the tribunal hearing must have been distressing for both parties and the outcome was to the advantage of neither. Tribunals are usually best avoided!

# 10 customer surprises

It's important to make sure that your customers know the rules by which you trade. Of course, rules are there to be bent. Here are ten ways in which your customers might surprise you.

1   **Lost deliveries** – always get deliveries signed for and the paperwork back from the carrier. It stops your customer's staff pinching goods and saying they never arrived.

2   **Rampant returns** – if a customer starts returning goods as 'faulty' it might be that they're not using them properly. Make time to visit and investigate.

3   **Cash crisis** – you deliver weekly and suddenly the customer is unable to pay. Do you keep supplying and hope they get back on track or pull out and cut your losses? Discuss!

4   **Legislation** – your customer points out that new legislation means you have to do something differently. Check that they're right, do it and pass on the cost.

5   **Relationships** – your salesperson has been sleeping with their buyer and the buyer's partner has just found out. You've probably lost a customer!

6   **Crime** – your fastest growing customer has been jailed for a serious crime. Can you help their team keep the business afloat or is it time to lower your risk and pull out?

7   **Complaints** – sometimes people complain because they're expecting too much. Provide specifications and application data sheets to define what you consider possible.

8   **Saying goodbye** – sometimes customers drop you for no good reason. Always ask why and act on their feedback if it's beneficial. Tell them what you've done as they might well return.

9   **Paying twice** – not every surprise is a nasty one. However, if a customer mistakenly pays twice, do send one payment back to demonstrate your honesty.

10  **Offering cash** – sometimes a customer offers to pay in cash. If they do, still put it through your books.

## Consultants

Consultants have to work harder than most to manage customer expectations. Here are some pitfalls that can trip up the hapless consultant.

● **You overpromised** – in the excitement of doing the deal, you agree to solve all their problems. It's not surprising they're unhappy that you've only solved three of them.

● **You did what they asked for, not what needed to be done** – consultancy is an area where you always have to look beyond the symptoms and work on the cause. If you don't think what you're being asked to do is going to work, you'll probably get the blame when it doesn't.

● **No terms of reference** – define the parameters of the project so that both parties understand. Only then can you be sure that you have finished the task.

● **One size doesn't fit all** – you've been on a course and want to deliver the same solution to all. All that happens is that you become blasé and clients feel ignored.

**brilliant** recap

The better you manage your customers' expectations, the fewer surprises you'll encounter. Customer problems are almost always the result of poor communication.

# 10 supplier surprises

Your suppliers may regard you as their best customer, but they will still let you down sometimes. Here are ten common surprises that suppliers can deliver to spoil your day.

1   **Lost deliveries** – goods really do go astray in transit and they cannot be replaced. Make sure you keep a buffer stock of all vital components.

2   **Quality drops** – if quality drops, work with your suppliers to resolve the problem. Visit them and see what is going wrong. Don't simply rant or change suppliers.

3   **Corporate deafness** – you've told them five times that something is wrong and they still keep doing it. This might mean it's time to find an alternative – you're no longer valued.

4   **Holidays** – make sure you know when suppliers are going on holiday and that you've got the gap covered. Many firms (for example, printers) shut down for holidays.

5   **Price rises** – it's funny how prices always rise and never fall. Ask for a reason why.

6   **Service stops** – if you stick with products that become outdated be aware that, unless you buy enough, your supplier might find it uneconomic to continue supplying you.

7   **Overengineering** – any product or service can be overengineered. New features are added and the price goes up. See if products can also be simplified and made cheaper.

8   **Legislation** – as with customers, the rules concerning suppliers can change and scupper what you've enjoyed for years. Watch the horizon for new regulations.

9   **Going bust** – sometimes suppliers go bust. Make sure you're not reliant on one supplier, and if the worst happens delay paying the last bill. Liquidators will often not pursue an insolvent company's creditors.

10  **Soured friendship** – be cautious of enjoying too much of your supplier's hospitality. Sometimes the friendship that develops compromises objectivity at work.

Choosing suppliers for your business is not as easy as you might think. Try to:

● look beyond the obvious local supplier that everyone else uses;

● buy on quality, innovation and service as well as price;

● take references from satisfied customers;

- let them make a profit too;
- write down the agreed 'service level agreement' so everyone understands.

Service level agreements sound grand but, in fact, are no more than documents that define:

- each aspect of the working relationship;
- what both parties have agreed to do;
- the penalties for failing to deliver;
- how both hope the relationship will develop;
- how success is reviewed and improvement sought.

 **example**

**Barry**

Although now retired, Barry tells a wonderful, if sobering, story from when he was site manager running a major agrochemical manufacturing plant. Being the only chemical plant in the city, there were no similar businesses nearby so some specialist suppliers were difficult to find locally.

One particular firm handled all of Barry's 'high pressure' stainless steel repair work and the plant became dependent on their quick, local service. The firm encountered financial problems and Barry was faced with possibly losing a key supplier. He arranged for some of his management team to work with the supplier through the difficult patch. The supplier survived and the relationship is now even closer.

# 10 unlikely but possible surprises

Surprises can come from many directions. Here are ten things that many never encounter – but if they come your way, this checklist will help you deal with them.

1   **Jury service** – if summoned to join a jury, you are usually allowed to be excused once if you really cannot spare the time. Most people never get called.

2   **Crime** – as long as you have a security system and are sensible then your business is unlikely to be attacked. Keep data back-ups offsite though, just in case.

3   **Poor health** – even the most severe flu epidemic is unlikely to affect everyone in your organisation at the same time. Experts suggest that at worst four out of five remain well.

4   **Hacking** – apart from credit card fraud you are unlikely to be of interest to hackers. They tend to target big organisations. Do have a firewall and don't visit suspect sites.

5   **Divorce** – remembering that divorce can cost you half your company and make domestic life far from comfortable, it makes sense to dedicate time and effort to keeping your relationship on an even keel.

6   **War** – all-out war is highly unlikely, although you do need to recognise that if you employ reservists, they could be called up for a tour of duty in places where Britain is fighting.

7   **Terrorism** – does your business operate in sensitive locations? If not, don't worry. If yes, then take advice. You're probably more at risk on public transport than at work.

8   **Bankruptcy** – you will probably find enough work for next month and there are umpteen stages of decline before financial apocalypse. Don't panic!

9   **Strikes** – even if your workers are ardent members of a trade union, industrial action is unlikely to disrupt your business if you are fair, open and honest.

10   **Death** – some people worry about dying and what would happen to the business. Relax – in this eventuality it's someone else's problem!

## Reality, fear and risk

In our dark moments, when tired, stressed and anxious, the world seems far more likely to deliver your enterprise a deadly blow than when you're on a high. Remember the following.

- Reality is:
  - where you are right now;
  - your perception of what is happening to those around you;
  - a world where, if you prioritise, you can make time to plan, think and react.
- Fear is:
  - irrational;
  - brought on by the anticipation of events you might possibly face;
  - delivered most often to those that invite it.
- Risk is:
  - measurable;
  - insurable;
  - manageable.

Focusing on risk is sensible when you are planning, but it can be damaging if you think about it all the time. Remember the 80:20 rule – spend most of your time on the 20 per cent of your activities/customers/products that carry 80 per cent of your opportunity.

 **brilliant    tip**

Life is as good as you make it. Don't spend all your time worrying about what might go wrong. Make the most of the moment and enjoy your success.

**CHAPTER 18**

# Be generous

How to help yourself by
helping others

# 10 ways to build your business by helping others

Read any large company's annual report and it will talk about 'corporate social responsibility'. Read further and you'll discover how this means they've been 'doing good', usually because it enhances their image. Increasingly, people running small businesses are discovering that social impact can deliver tangible returns. Here are ten ways to market your business by 'doing good'.

1　**Mentor** – develop your management skills and see your own business through the eyes of someone else. Mentor someone managing a voluntary or community organisation. You'll learn from each other.

2　**Give away products** – if you make a consumer product, give away a redundant product to someone who would not normally be able to buy or use it. Make sure you get news coverage.

3　**Share knowledge** – share your experience and advice with people starting a business from a disadvantaged background. The Prince's Trust is one organisation that can help you do this. Get to know the other mentors; they could be potential customers for you.

4　**Offer work experience** – it's not just kids that need work experience. People rebuilding their confidence after mental ill health also need reintroducing to the world of work. Providing work experience shows that you care. People prefer to trade with people who care.

5　**Host visits** – allow others to see how you run your organisation. The visit will inevitably be promoted to a wide audience and many who come will be potential customers.

6　**Share scrap** – if you make things, your waste materials or packaging could be useful to a social enterprise that reuses materials. Reduce your costs and increase your profile.

7　**Teach kids** – explaining what you do and why to a group of 13-year-olds is a great experience. It will certainly make you think because kids ask lots of questions and demand credible answers. It's good to have your basic assumptions challenged.

8　**Raise money** – if you employ people, get them to agree on a local good cause and help them to raise funds as a team. There are lots of things to do. It really motivates a team.

9   **Put a bench outside your shop** – make it possible for people to rest outside your shop. It makes it look busier and everyone will look in the window.

10  **Sponsor people** – funding the youth football team's shirts and printing your firm's name on the back is perhaps the most obvious way of trading support for publicity.

As soon as you recognise that your business forms part of a wider society, you begin to see that the opportunities are endless. The concept of helping to raise your organisation's profile through helping others is perhaps a little more complex than many of the topics in this book. It is, however, not to be overlooked. To illustrate the point, here are some specific examples of things that have been done before.

| Activity | Benefit to the business |
|---|---|
| A baker gives leftover cakes to a hostel for rough sleepers | Everyone knows that the cakes they buy in the morning really are freshly baked |
| An accountant runs free advice sessions for start-up businesses | This is the first accountant the new entrepreneur meets – they get to meet lots of potential new clients |
| An ad agency does all the marketing for a city charity appeal for nothing | The campaign is widely seen and wins an award – the agency wins work from bigger charities with budgets to invest |
| An engineering works allows a local college to train students in its workshops after hours | The firm can look for potential employees and all become familiar with their workplace |
| An IT company helps in a school | Parents hear about this and may buy from them |

## brilliant   recap

We all prefer to do business with nice people. Therefore, by doing nice things for others, your own popularity and success will increase.

# 10 ways to entertain your customers for free

Creating social opportunities to bond with those who we want to do business with can be difficult. Many prefer not to accept corporate gifts and the days of lavish lunches are long past. Here are ten very appropriate, free or cheap ways to entertain customers.

1   **Fund-raising dinners** – people will buy tickets for a dinner if some of the money goes to a good cause. People will also be more likely to attend!

2   **Join a club** – even if you are not into 'gentleman's clubs' you can join something that provides appropriate hospitality opportunities. For example, friends of art galleries can often take guests to exhibitions for free.

3   **Ask them to pay!** – if they recognise that you have pared your costs to the bone and have made only a modest profit, then why shouldn't they buy lunch for you?

4   **Supplier seminars** – get your suppliers to organise seminars for your customers. Make sure they include food and drink, as well as time to network and socialise.

5   **Trade body events** – take your customers to hear industry pundits speak at trade events.

6   **Recognise achievement** – give an award for excellence in your field. Invite others to the presentation. Have the buffet sponsored by your bank.

7   **Take them on a walk** – perhaps not viewed by all as entertaining, but why not encourage your customers to join you in a sponsored walk? Get tired together!

8   **Hijack a trade seminar** – organise your own 'fringe' programme around an event you and your customers are attending. It's cheaper than doing it on your own.

9   **Travel together** – people seem reluctant to share cars yet offering a lift to those you want to influence, when you are both going to a trade show for example, converts travelling time into selling time.

10  **Give kittens** – if your cat surprises you by having kittens, invite your business contacts to provide good homes for them. You'll always then have a good reason to phone.

Fund-raising events can create fantastic opportunities to bring together customers, prospects, suppliers and others important to your success. As suggested in the checklist above, those you invite will buy their ticket and pay their way. They might also provide raffle and tombola prizes. These events take a lot of organising and the benefiting good cause should be able to help.

Here are some other benefits of fund-raising events.

- Big name speakers will often waive their fee if they approve of the cause.
- People will come to network with each other – they will talk positively about you.
- Guests of guests are often people you've never met.
- You get plenty of profile and get to speak to everyone.
- The presentation of the cheque may be featured in your local or trade press.
- Following up to ask if people enjoyed themselves can lead to talking business.
- Others may sponsor certain elements of the event so you can raise more money.
- Sharing the event with a non-competitor lets you influence each other's networks.
- Invitations can carry subtle advertising.
- Everyone thinks you're a generous person – this makes business easier to do.

## brilliant example

**The Tate, www.tate.org.uk**

London is well served by member-only business clubs. The Institute of Directors is a good example and The Hospital Club in Soho is another. Both charge annual membership fees and provide a place to meet customers and drink coffee or eat lunch. Both are more select than meeting in Starbucks.

Few people, however, consider holding their business meetings at an art gallery such as the Tate. Membership of the Tate costs less than most business clubs, yet the benefits are greater. Not only do London's Tate museums have member-only cafes, but you can also take your guests for a stroll through any current exhibitions without having to buy tickets.

Meeting at the Tate also helps you differentiate yourself from other entrepreneurs.

## brilliant recap

You don't have to entertain your customers lavishly to win their support. Most realise that they are, in reality, funding any extravagance. There really is no such thing as a free lunch!

# 10 lessons you can learn from social entrepreneurs

Social enterprises are special. They are also a fast-growing business sector. There are many definitions but, in a nutshell, a successful social enterprise has a social purpose that is equal to or greater than its profit motive. Here are ten things you can learn from social enterprises.

1   **Passion** – they are usually started by people wishing to bring about lasting social change. Their passion and desire to do good gives them immense determination and strength.

2   **Access to funding** – set up a social enterprise and you can seek funding from some grant-making trusts as well as from the bank. You have more flexibility.

3   **Transparency** – if formally registered as a 'community interest company' with Companies House, a social enterprise is bound to invest most of its profits in its social goals. How can you make your commitment to others equally transparent?

4   **Customer appeal** – if you match the service offered by a global brand of, say, a coffee shop, then people will often choose you first if you have a strong social or ethical focus.

5   **More sustainable** – social enterprises are commercial and thus able to choose their path without too much influence from funders who might have different priorities.

6   **Bridging the gap** – a charity and 'for profit' business can set up a jointly owned social enterprise, pooling skills and sharing the return. It's a unique opportunity.

7   **More motivated staff** – in general, people choose to work for a social enterprise because they share the values. Everyone sees it as much as a vocation as a job.

8   **Less competition** – there are fewer social enterprises and they are different from 'for profit' businesses. Because you are 'different', you encounter less direct market competition.

9   **You can reward yourself** – charity rules can make it difficult to reward yourself. Set up a social enterprise and the rules allow you to pay salaries and dividends.

10   **Being green** – because you are not just about making money, it's easier to make sure that you follow good environmental practice. You can set a good example for others to follow.

By their very nature, social enterprises can be easier to set up than 'for profit' businesses. This is because they can attract 'pump priming' grants. Investors also take a longer-term view. Here are some opportunities you may spot if you establish a social enterprise.

- **Venture philanthropists** – people who lend money to social enterprises on more favourable terms than if you were setting up a 'for profit' business.

- **Rent holidays** – public sector landlords, in particular, may give you a rent holiday to make it easier to establish your social enterprise.

- **Business support** – people already established may be inclined to give you practical support, discounted services and more.

- **Grants** – if you partner a charity they may have access to capital grants that can fund your set-up costs. Unlike loans, grants don't have to be repaid.

- **Invitations to share resources** – neighbouring organisations may well offer to share stuff with you.

To succeed as a social entrepreneur you need to be able to clearly demonstrate that you are focused, businesslike and objective. If people view you as a woolly minded idealist, they will not give you their support.

## brilliant example

**Fifteen, www.fifteen.net**

Perhaps one of the UK's best-known social enterprises, Fifteen was set up by TV chef Jamie Oliver to enable disadvantaged young people to gain the confidence, skills and experience to work in the restaurant trade.

Named after the initial cohort of 15 trainees, the enterprise invests the profits made in the restaurants in developing and supporting the trainees. Fifteen does not compromise the quality of its food or service. Despite much of the food diners eat being prepared by trainees, it is able to command premium prices.

By working to very high standards the restaurants can make good profits and help more trainees. Fifteen illustrates how an ambitious social enterprise can deliver to the highest standards.

# 10 benefits of making a philanthropic gesture

Many of the world's most successful entrepreneurs have set up their own charitable foundations. This enables them to make a difference in the world by sharing their fortunes with those who are less fortunate. You're probably not a multimillionaire, but that doesn't mean you can't afford to be philanthropic. Here are ten good reasons to share your profits with others.

1    **Feel good** – using the proceeds of your success to help others makes you feel good.

2    **Lasting** – however well known you have become in your business sector, you will eventually be forgotten. Giving can make sure you are remembered.

3    **Tax** – you need to take advice but giving to charitable causes is incredibly tax efficient.

4    **Children** – of course you want to give your children a good start. But give them too much and you may spoil them. Get them to help you choose the causes you support.

5    **How much is enough?** – when you've made sufficient to realise your life's dreams, the rest just becomes an investment portfolio you worry about. Give away what you won't miss.

6    **World changing** – governments can never make as big a difference as an individual. They don't have your focus, passion or drive. You can respond quickly to need.

7    **Direct action** – don't just lobby for a new playground for your local school – build one!

8    **Vital** – some sectors – for example, the arts – rely on patronage to survive.

9    **Recognition** – if this is important to you, most major gifts can be publicly acknowledged. Anonymity is preferred by some, public acclaim by others. Both are equally valid.

10   **Preservation** – for things that might otherwise be lost for ever. It is a fact that increasingly it is only philanthropy that keeps many worthwhile projects running.

If you want to avoid the flood of begging letters that becoming philanthropic can prompt, consider giving money via a community foundation. Most places have one. You then simply give them the money and they invite groups to bid for grants. They are professional and can assess applications impartially. You can choose to remain part of that grant-making process.

Here are some philanthropy ideas to get you started.

| Area | Low budget | Medium budget | Massive budget |
|---|---|---|---|
| Education | Buy books for local school | Sponsor a curriculum area | Build a school |
| | Provide an item of equipment | Equip a laboratory | Fund a university chair |
| Health | Provide a TV for the doctor's waiting room | Fund a specialist clinic | Build a hospice |
| | Provide an item of specialist equipment | Support work overseas | Build a medical mission |
| Arts | Pay for art therapy | Fund an arts worker | Build a gallery |
| | Sponsor an exhibition | Fund an 'artist in residence' | Fund a monument |

 **example**

**Andy Rackham, APR Telecoms, www.aprtelecoms.co.uk**

After being made redundant in the 1990s, Andy set up his own company selling and maintaining telephone systems. Over the years the business grew and diversified. As the company got larger, so it became increasingly important to maintain a high profile in the business community his business served.

When it came to making charitable donations Andy chose to join a network of business owners making regular donations to his local community foundation. Andy does not shout about his giving as it is driven by personal not business motives. However, those who are close enough to the organisation to know about his giving are quite likely to recommend his firm. They know that, as with any donor, the more successful they become, the more they are able to give.

**CHAPTER 19**

# Sell your business

How to realise the value

# 10 ways to decide that it's time to move on

Businesses have a natural lifespan. It's often best to sell up before they reach a point where dramatic change is needed to avoid decline. Here are ten signs that indicate it's time to sell and move on.

1   **You get an offer** – someone else has spotted the potential and perhaps has the energy and enthusiasm you used to have. Or maybe they want to add your business to theirs? Think about it!

2   **You're bored** – it happens. The business is no longer exciting and the problems seem to be greater than the opportunities. You need a change – and so too does your business.

3   **You're old** – why work longer than you really need? If your business is worth enough to fund a long and happy retirement, why not cash in and develop new interests?

4   **Investment is needed** – to stay competitive you need major investment and it would make more sense to become part of a larger organisation. You need to acquire or be acquired.

5   **Market is maturing** – you've had the best years and now it's time to adapt or perish. Alternatively, sell while there's still some market left.

6   **Big players** – you've started in a niche market and grown to the point that the big players are getting annoyed. Maybe they'd like to buy you out? Ask them.

7   **Opportunity knocks** – there's a great 'once in a lifetime' chance to get involved with something new. If you're sure it's not merely a case of the 'grass looking greener', then sell to release time and cash – but don't rush on either front.

8   **Eager beavers** – your successor, whom you've been grooming for years, is snapping at your heels. You may need to allow a management buyout now or risk losing your in-house buyer.

9   **Pressure at home** – has your partner retired already? If so, it's not unreasonable for them to want you to do the same. Remember that good relationships are worth more than business success.

10  **You just want to** – if it feels right and you're sure it's what you want to do, and if you're the majority shareholder, then it's your prerogative to call the shots.

When people buy a small business, they often try to commit the owner to staying on to make sure that the value in the business is retained. In other words, they want you to stay around, perhaps even for a year, to keep the customers, staff and suppliers loyal. If this doesn't appeal to you, make sure your business can run smoothly without you before you seek a buyer.

There are a number of ways of selling a business. It's not often as straightforward as someone writing you a large cheque! Here are some examples.

- **Cash up front** – you get paid and walk away. This is the ideal, but it rarely happens!
- **Earn out** – you are paid from future income. This often happens when professional practices are purchased. It links the price to client retention.
- **Shares** – you get paid in shares and end up owning part of the parent company. Unless it's stock market listed, those shares may be difficult to sell. On the other hand, you could end up with a fortune.

## brilliant example

**Gail and Stuart Shreeve, www.cursonconsultants.com**

In 1990 husband and wife team Gail and Stuart Shreeve spotted the opportunity to make more thermally efficient refrigerated van conversions. They set up a small workshop and over the next 18 years grew a very successful business. Innovative design, high-quality workmanship and personal service, together with a proactive 'can do' approach to their business, enabled them to become market leaders.

In 2008 they were approached by a competitor seeking to expand. Not yet old enough to retire, they decided to accept the offer and set up a consultancy. Today they are growing their new business, using their considerable expertise but free of the headaches and challenges that inevitably punctuated their lives when running a busy workshop. Both they and the team who bought their company are very happy with how things have turned out.

# 10 things that add value to your business

Business transfer agents and accountants apply all sorts of formulae to value a business. The reality is that for most people the price you get when you sell is the price that someone is prepared to pay. Here are ten business value boosters.

1   **Profits** – the ability to make good profits consistently is the most important factor in establishing a business's value.

2   **Potential** – the second most important factor is hard evidence that profits will continue to grow. What indicators are there that the future looks even better than the past?

3   **People** – if you've employed and motivated really good people and you hardly need to visit the office, your business is worth more than if you've been a control freak.

4   **Premises** – is your business operating from a location that's worth more than the business itself? If your cycle repair shop could be bulldozed to make way for a supermarket, get excited!

5   **Intellectual property** – any patents or trade marks need to be registered so that your buyer knows that those intangible assets are fully protected.

6   **Loyal customers** – customer inertia has a huge value. If much of your business is repeat business then a buyer can confidently expect those customers to remain loyal.

7   **Reputation** – if you've worked hard to maintain a high profile in your target market, you probably have a good reputation. Reputation does affect value.

8   **Market position** – if you command a price premium then your business is less susceptible to a market downturn. Being in the top third of your sector is worth more than being cheapest.

9   **Location** – some businesses are easy to relocate while others need to be where they are. Location is important, as is room to grow and a ready source of potential employees.

10  **Your motivation** – if you've lost the plot then your business will be worth less than if you're still out there fighting the business battle. It's best to quit while you're ahead!

## Profits versus value

Your business gives you a good income and a pleasing degree of control over how your spend your time. To be honest though, many can achieve this as an employee, so the question is, why are you in business? The right answer is to create an enterprise that you can sell. This means that, at some point in the future, you can swap the overdraft for a pile of cash.

As you build your business you should never lose sight of the need to add value and create an enterprise (or enterprises) that can be sold one day. This should be the carrot at the end of your stick. There are some personal qualities you need to develop if you are to build real value into your business. These include:

- **objectivity** – you must let your head run your business, not your heart;
- **focus** – stick to what you do best and do it better – avoid distraction;
- **separation** – the business is your baby but you need to give it room to be independent of you – don't muddle up what's yours and what's the firm's.

## What's worth the most?

When someone buys your business, they will attach the greatest value to the elements of the business that can give them the biggest return. For example, if buying your garden centre enables a chain of garden centres to fill a gap in their coverage of the area, they might pay over the odds to take you over. This is because:

- they'll spread the acquisition costs over the whole group turnover;
- they might already be generating interest from their advertising that cannot be met in your area – buying you means they increase their return on marketing;
- your planning consent and infrastructure mean they can trade far sooner than if they developed their own 'green field' site.

 **recap**

People buy potential and performance, not your personal passion!

# 10 ways to find a buyer

Ideally you want to market your business discreetly, rather than hanging a 'for sale' sign on the door. Here are ten ways to sell without making it obvious.

1  **Ask the accountant** – some accountants specialise in matchmaking between sellers and buyers of small businesses. They recruit buyers through seminars and local knowledge, and then broker the deal.

2  **Chat to suppliers** – if you sit between your suppliers and the marketplace, they might be interested in buying you out. Start the chat with 'Just suppose . . .'.

3  **Chat to big customers** – if you are a vital supplier to a customer, it might appeal to them to diversify and take control of your firm. It could strengthen their position.

4  **Ask the team** – you will know your people well. Are they likely to be able to put together a management buyout? For many smaller firms this is the best way to sell.

5  **Use box numbers** – you've seen the ads in the paper. They describe the business vaguely and give a box number for enquiries. It's cheap enough, so try it!

6  **Alert rising stars** – who's the wunderkind in your sector? More importantly, who is backing them? Let it be known that you might be receptive to merger talks.

7  **Approach the competition** – if you've grown to a size where you are annoying a far larger competitor, they may well be willing to buy you out to regain market control.

8  **Through agents** – as with houses and commercial property, there are agents who specialise in selling businesses. They are good at attracting potential buyers.

9  **Through an insolvency practitioner** – if things are not going well and you're really bailing out, an insolvency practitioner can often help you to plan a clean escape by selling your business.

10  **Network** – put yourself about and listen to what people say. Don't attend networking events to promote that you want to sell, more to see what intelligence you can glean.

Working out what your business is worth has already been covered. It is essentially all about its potential to deliver future returns to the new owner. Your business will be worth more to someone who wants:

- **to buy it for emotional reasons** – for example, someone retiring with plans to run a B&B;
- **to plug a gap** – in their regional, national or international network;
- **more control** – of the market or supply chain;
- **your people** – because they have valuable skills;
- **your customers** – because winning them 'in battle' might cost more.

Selling up is not a quick process. It usually takes several months from the time you find your buyer to the cheque arriving. The buyer will want to delve deeply into your business's affairs, usually accompanied by professional advisers. Make sure you have at least your accountant helping you through the process.

After you have sold your business, you should never:

- dwell on the deal and question your decision;
- be envious if the business suddenly takes off;
- be smug if it consequently goes bust;
- compete with your former company;
- speak badly of the new team.

# 10 reasons to merge your business with another

One way to grow quickly, as well as to create your own exit route, is to merge your business with another. When merging, always make sure you consider these ten points.

1   **You'll get on** – if you are going to stay with the merged business you need to be sure you'll get on with your new business partners.

2   **2 + 2 = 5** – there has to be a clear benefit, either in terms of additional skills or reduced overhead costs. If 2 + 2 = 4, don't do it.

3   **Bigger is better** – if you are a minnow among sharks then getting bigger quickly can protect you both from being gobbled up.

4   **The figures add up** – take professional advice from your accountant, who will also check out the deal and protect your interests. Accept that this will be frustrating!

5   **Compliance costs** – some professional practices face ever-mounting compliance costs. Joining two together means you can share these costs. It's a good reason to merge.

6   **Knowledge base** – almost the opposite of compliance, but arguably more important in a fast-changing sector such as law or architecture. Sharing your knowledge with others means both less spent and more learned.

7   **Customer overlap** – you supply the same people with different things. Merging means you have lots more time to find and service additional business.

8   **Premises** – your lease is running out and the other concern has space available.

9   **Plant** – merging means you can buy one big efficient machine to do the work of two smaller inefficient ones. You both benefit from the economies of scale.

10  **You know the full story** – you need to be sure there are no skeletons in the cupboard.

When you merge your business with another, only one person will remain top dog – businesses with two bosses rarely work. It will help therefore if one of the advantages of merging is that those leading the new business have complementary skills. One firm, for example, might be led by an accomplished salesperson who can win lots of new business. The other might be more delivery focused with the leader being an engineer or professional practitioner.

When merging two businesses you also need to check the following.

- **Employment contracts** – you will need to produce one that suits both teams.
- **Pay levels** – often these are different and you will need to have parity.
- **Culture** – take the best of both businesses when creating the new one.
- **Your bank** – consult them before doing the deal and make sure they are supportive.
- **Customers** – make sure that key customers are happy with what's planned.
- **Suppliers** – rationalise your list to retain the most supportive.
- **Employment law** – if there are to be casualties, they should be dealt with fairly and in line with current best practice.
- **Guarantees** – make sure that you are sharing financial commitments fairly.
- **Perks** – if the other owner has a Porsche 'on the firm' and your car is more modest, you will need to eliminate the danger of future disagreements.
- **Advisers** – if you have different advisers, collectively choose one to stick with after the merger.

# 10 things you'll do differently the second time around

When you've sold your business, the first thing you'll want is a long holiday. Then you might decide to put into practice all you've learned and do it all again, either in the same business sector or in a completely fresh one. Here are ten ways in which your second business will probably be different from the first.

1  **More objective** – you'll be less idealistic and more focused on the business itself. Serial entrepreneurs are usually more stimulated by the business performance than by the business activity.

2  **More people-focused** – the best businesses are those with the best people. Motivating others to deliver your vision is always easier the second time. You know how to recruit better.

3  **Tougher** – we learn from our mistakes. You're tougher and can weather the storms more easily.

4  **More compassionate** – being aware of where others are trying to go makes you more tolerant and more willing to compromise a little. You are also older and wiser.

5  **Better funded** – you can afford to invest more the second time. That helps all round.

6  **Better networked** – you know people and people know you. It's easier when you have an established network. Your reputation will help you succeed sooner.

7  **Buy better** – you know how to buy and what to look for. You won't get ripped off.

8  **Sell more** – already successful, you have the confidence and skill to sell more successfully than you did when you first started out.

9  **Play harder** – you've perhaps enjoyed a sabbatical and appreciate the value of quality time. Life is more balanced this time round.

10  **Quit quicker** – you'll build value faster and make your exit sooner.

Most businesses in the UK are small with annual sales of less than £150,000. Only a few experience the runaway success that can deliver vast riches. Running a small business is as much a career as a quest for wealth. As with a career, you will go further faster if you:

- **move often** – selling, learning and starting again is the fastest way to grow;
- **delegate** – focus more on strategy and less on operational issues;
- **stay clean** – do not tarnish your reputation;
- **help others** – it's odd but the more you help others, the better you do yourself;
- **enjoy it** – making work fun also makes it easier – this goes for your team too!

Really successful people often build a portfolio of businesses. These will include companies that they:

- **invest in** – and support the executive team to achieve the vision;
- **own** – but which are entirely managed by trusted employees;
- **advise** – where they give their expertise freely and learn too;
- **admire** – in which they have a small role but derive much pleasure;
- **respect** – and want to help to succeed.

To keep developing your skills as an entrepreneur you should now:

- scan business books and journals and read what's best for you;
- help others, for they in return will want to help you;
- listen to reputable business speakers and ask them probing questions;
- keep a diary so that you can look back and learn from what you did;
- create a training plan for yourself and be prepared to invest in good courses.

CHAPTER 20

# Useful document templates

Shortcuts for you to copy,
adapt and use

# Sales letters

You use sales letters to make an approach to people you think might be interested in the products or services you offer. It is more direct than advertising and can give you a better response. Here are ten important things to consider when writing sales letters.

1   **Targeting** – sales letters are not direct mail. It's better to send a few well-aimed letters than distribute thousands of poorly targeted, impersonal ones.

2   **Research** – the more you can find out about the person you are writing to, the more likely it is that they will read your letter. Use the internet to research your prospects.

3   **Personalise** – people get lots of junk mail. Your letter has to be quickly seen as 'something else'. Make the letter obviously personal to the recipient.

4   **Familiarity** – older people prefer to be addressed as Mr or Mrs. Younger people are happy to be addressed as 'Dear first name'. Don't be overly familiar or too formal.

5   **Short** – the best sales letters are short and to the point. Keep to one page.

6   **Specific** – make it very clear what you are offering and why you think it's appropriate to your target. Tell them in clear terms why you have written to them. Do not use the tactic employed by large mailing houses who use phrases like 'you have been selected for'.

7   **Say what you want** – there has to be a simple call to action. Don't use euphemisms – say it like it is.

8   **Don't ask too much** – your sales letter is written to open dialogue with your prospect. People don't buy from sales letters – they simply respond to an invitation to know more.

9   **Sign it yourself** – always sign your sales letters personally and don't use black ink. If you do, people will assume it's been printed rather than handwritten.

10  **Offer choices** – let people choose how to respond. Enclose a reply envelope and provide a phone number. Offering choice increases the response rate.

## Sample sales letter

Dear Mr Smith

I was browsing classic car websites the other day and noticed that you are secretary of the Anytown Triumph Herald Club. Classic cars are an interest of mine, although I have yet to buy one of my own.

My company provides embroidered shirts, baseball caps and other promotional merchandise to sports and social clubs of all kinds. I wondered if your club members would like the opportunity to wear clothing that carries your club name and logo.

Some of the clubs we serve sell our products to raise funds for the club. Others choose to sell them to members at cost because they like members to 'fly the flag' at meetings and events.

We would be delighted to work with you to design and provide garments and merchandise that your members will value and enjoy. If you could fill in and return the short questionnaire I have enclosed, I will willingly produce you a sample T-shirt without obligation. Alternatively, give me a ring if you have any specific needs or ideas you would like to discuss.

I look forward to hearing from you.

Yours sincerely

Steven Stitch

## Sales letter structure

1   Name your prospect to make the letter personal.

2   Explain how you got their name and why you're writing.

3   Say what you do and why it's relevant.

4   Ask the recipient to do something and offer alternatives.

5   Sign it with your first name and family name.

6   If you promise an enclosure, don't forget to put it in!

# Follow-up letters

Once you've established two-way communication with your prospect or customer, you need to keep in touch. Don't pester them, but write whenever there's a specific opportunity you think would appeal to them. Here are ten examples.

1    **It's been a while** – you've written about some offer but there's been no response. It's been proven that sending up to two follow-up letters can prompt purchase. People often simply put your letter to one side or forget. No reply doesn't always mean no interest.

2    **Their next service is due** – if you maintain equipment for your customer, take the initiative and write to tell them when the next service is due.

3    **Good news** – you've just won a business award. Write and tell your customers and include a 'celebratory' offer. Equally, write it so that they win an award too!

4    **Deadlines** – we all live with them. Write to your customers when you know a significant deadline is looming. This also applies to seasonal businesses.

5    **Referral letter** – a new customer has suggested some people you might contact. Break the ice with a letter of introduction that names the person who referred them.

6    **They said no last time** – if you lose an order, wait a while and then write to ask how they're getting on with the new supplier. Things might not be working out. You need to know.

7    **You saw them in the paper** – everyone loves being pictured in the newspaper. Write to congratulate them and then introduce your offer. Few others will do this.

8    **You've got a new product** – give existing customers the chance to preview new products. It makes them feel that they are important to you.

9    **You want to delegate** – as your business grows, you will want to pass some customers on to your team. Do this by letter of introduction – it avoids their feeling dumped.

10    **You're fund-raising** – it may be your job to raise money. Equally, you might simply be looking for sponsors for your first marathon. Write to your supporters and they may support you more.

## Sample follow-up letter

Dear Mr Smith

It's been three months since your last purchase of our multivitamin tablets for your dog. I hope that your pet is well and that you have seen an improvement in health, vitality and condition as a result of adding our products to your animal's feed.

By our calculations you must be ready for another consignment soon. Would you like me to post some to you? The price remains the same as before, £25.00 for a box of 500 tablets. Postage and packing is free. I enclose a ready completed order form and reply paid envelope for your convenience. Alternatively you can phone or reorder via our website.

I also enclose information about our new lines of pet care products. Many customers have been asking us to widen our range and we have been happy to oblige. You can add any of these to your next order and we will cover the cost of postage.

I look forward to hearing from you.

Yours sincerely

Steven Stitch

## Follow-up letter structure

1   Name your customer to make the letter personal.
2   Explain why you're writing – make it specific.
3   Spell out what it's going to cost and don't miss a new sales opportunity.
4   Make it easy to respond.
5   Sign it with your first name and family name.
6   If you promise an enclosure, don't forget to put it in!

# Getting-paid letters

You've done the deal and sent the invoice. Now you need to make sure you get paid. Here are ten steps to getting your money, however reluctant the customer is to pay!

1   **Make sure your invoice is correct** – incorrect invoices can get stuck in the customer's accounts department. Make sure it's accurate and quotes their order number.

2   **Send a statement** – some people pay only on receipt of a statement. Send one at the end of each month to summarise recent transactions.

3   **Pick up the phone** – if the money's overdue, ring and ask for it. Find out what the problem is. If there is no problem, you need to move on to step 4.

4   **Write a letter** – be firm and polite and make it clear when you expect to be paid.

5   **Send a second letter** – express disappointment that you've not seen payment and say that you will take legal action if the money is not with you by a certain date.

6   **Post a copy of your completed Small Claims Court form** – this shows that you are serious (small claims are those less than £5000). Write to give one more week to pay.

7   **Start court proceedings** – the court then writes to your debtor and many pay at this point. They also have to pay your court fee.

8   **Attend the hearing** – small claims are heard by a judge in his office. It is relatively informal and the judge will be friendly and fair. You are face to face with your debtor.

9   **If you win the hearing** – your debtor will be required to pay you, perhaps by instalments.

10  **If you lose the hearing** – reflect on why this happened. Was there any fault on your side? Did you fail to prepare your argument for the judge? Be honest with yourself.

## Sample getting-paid letter

Dear Mr Smith

Despite sending you a statement and phoning your office to speak to you, it appears you have still not settled my invoice number 1234 (a copy of which I enclose). You have not given me any reason why you have chosen not to pay for the bricks we delivered to your site on 18 March and I must insist that you send me a cheque by return.

We accept credit cards, so if it would be more convenient to spread your payments using your credit card to settle our invoice we would allow that. You do, however, need to call into our depot to do this.

I am very sorry that you have not managed to find time either to pay this invoice or to speak with me when I phoned. I feel we have no alternative but to start a Small Claims Court action against you should your money not be in our bank by the end of the month.

I look forward to hearing from you.

Yours sincerely

Brian Brickmaker

## Getting-paid letter structure

1 Name your debtor and be polite – avoid sarcasm.

2 Outline the steps that you've already taken and enclose a copy invoice.

3 Explain what you will do if the money is not forthcoming. Offer a choice if you can.

4 End by expressing your sorrow at the situation.

5 If you promise an enclosure, don't forget to put it in!

# The business plan

There is a checklist to help you prepare your business plan on page 41. Here though is an example of how the information can be presented on one page.

My one-page business plan – the Red Bus

| My objectives | My goals | To make this happen I need to | And I'll do these first |
|---|---|---|---|
| What we do | Income/profit<br>Sales this year: £50,000<br>Sales next year: £150,000<br>Sales in 3 years' time: £400,000 | • Carry more passengers<br>• Make more money from each one<br>• Encourage more people to travel by bus | • Change my timetable<br>• Add some new routes<br>• Join an environmental party |
| Who we do it for | Customers   No.   Spend p.a.<br>This year:   1000   £50<br>Next year:   2000   £75<br>In 3 years'<br>time:       3000   £133 | • Sell newspapers<br>• Start to do excursions<br>• Do weekend breaks | • Open a wholesale newspaper account<br>• Build a list of clubs and societies<br>• Explore hotels that will give me a deal |
| What makes us money? | Products/services<br>This year: One bus<br>Next year: One bigger bus<br>In 3 years' time: One bus plus one coach | • Trade in my bus for a bigger one<br>• Start looking for a coach<br>• Buy a coach in two years' time | • Start reading *Bus Weekly*<br>• Visit a coach exhibition<br>• Find out about finance |
| Where it's leading? | Investment<br>This year I need £5000<br>Next year I need £20,000<br>In 3 years' time I'll need £80,000 | • Find more working capital<br>• Find a leasing company to fund the bus/coach<br>• Plan an advertising budget | • Talk to my bank and others<br>• Join a business network<br>• Talk to marketing firms |
| What's in it for me? | People<br>This year I employ:<br>Next year I need:<br>In 3 years' time I'll have: | • Employ part-time drivers<br>• Employ four part-time drivers<br>• Employ one full-time and five part-time drivers | • Find out what other firms pay<br>• Build a list of good drivers<br>• Ask my two drivers who they know |

# Confidentiality and intellectual property

You are right to be concerned about protecting what is yours from those who might copy it. If the stakes are high, you should never cut corners but hire the best professionals you can afford. For those seeking a quick fix, here's a checklist and a draft disclosure agreement.

1   **Be pragmatic** – you can take this stuff too seriously. Remember that the cost of litigation is so high that having agreements, trade marks and patents is only half the story. Defending your rights against a large, well-resourced opponent can be prohibitive.

2   **Mind who you show** – if you've developed something new then talk to a patent agent before you show it to anyone else. Once you've shown others, it can prove impossible to patent.

3   © – add this symbol to everything you publish. It simply asserts that you are claiming it as copyright.

4   ™ – this abbreviation for 'trade mark' can be added to any logo or symbol you consider your own. You don't need to register it to do this, just add a superscript ™ to any print.

5   ® – this symbol means you have a registered trade mark. You need to consult a trade mark lawyer (or be very clever) to get trade marks registered.

6   **Non-disclosure agreements** – these are most frequently used when you are showing a potential associate or supplier the details of something you plan to protect by patent. Remember that you cannot patent what you have publicly disclosed.

7   **Patents** – these are listed on national patent registers. You need a patent agent to help you file a patent as the process is lengthy and complex. You can search the UK register of patents by following the link to 'find patents' at **http://www.ipo.gov.uk/patent.htm**.

8   **Domain names** – always remember that search engines look for website content – the name of your domain is not as important as you might think. That said, it does make sense to have a domain name that links to your business or product name. Search to see what is available at **http://www.whois.org/**.

9   **Business name** – if you're going to be a sole trader, you can pretty much choose whatever name you wish. Legally you will be 'John Smith trading as Acme Carpets' or similar. However, to avoid confusion, make sure you research carefully and do

not choose a name that may get you confused with someone else. You can register almost any trading name as a trade mark, providing that someone else hasn't registered it already!

10 **Perspective** – your approach to trade marks, patents and the like will largely be dictated by your ambition. If you are setting out to beat the world, you need to invest in the best possible advice because much of the value of your business may rest in its intellectual property. If, on the other hand, you simply want to enjoy life and be comfortable, this might not be quite so vital to your continued success. Be realistic and keep things in perspective.

## Sample non-disclosure letter

CONFIDENTIAL DISCLOSURE AGREEMENT

Between: [company name and address]
and: [your name and address]

1. On the understanding that both parties are interested in meeting to consider possible collaboration in developments arising from [your name]'s intellectual property, it is agreed that all information, oral, written or otherwise, that is supplied in the course or as a result of such meeting shall be treated as confidential by the receiving party.

2. The receiving party undertakes not to use the information for any purpose, other than for the purpose of considering the said collaboration, without obtaining the written agreement of the disclosing party.

3. This Agreement applies to both technical and commercial information communicated by either party.

4. This Agreement does not apply to any information in the public domain or which the receiving party can show was either already lawfully in their possession prior to its disclosure by the other party or acquired without the involvement, either directly or indirectly, of the disclosing party.

5. Either party to this Agreement shall on request from the other return any documents or items connected with the disclosure and shall not retain any unauthorised copies or likenesses.

▶

6.   This Agreement, or the supply of information referred to in paragraph 1, does not create any licence, title or interest in respect of any intellectual property rights of the disclosing party.

7.   After [numerals] years from the date hereof each party shall be relieved of all obligations under this Agreement.

Signed: [your signature]

For: [your business/trading name if relevant]

Date:

NOTE: This sample document is just that, a sample. It was reproduced from 'A Better Mousetrap: the Business of Invention' published by online invention consultancy **www.abettermousetrap.co.uk**.